REPRESENTATION in CHILDREN'S LITERATURE

T0368934

REPRESENTATION iN CHILDREN'S LITERATURE

REFLECTING REALITIES IN THE CLASSROOM BY THE CENTRE FOR LITERACY IN PRIMARY EDUCATION

with **Farrah Serroukh**

1 Oliver's Yard
55 City Road
London EC1Y 1SP

2455 Teller Road
Thousand Oaks
California 91320

Unit No 323-333, Third Floor, F-Block
International Trade Tower
Nehru Place, New Delhi – 110 019

8 Marina View Suite 43-053
Asia Square Tower 1
Singapore 018960

Editor: Amy Thornton
Senior project editor: Chris Marke
Cover design: Wendy Scott
Typeset by: C&M Digitals (P) Ltd, Chennai, India
Printed and bound by CPI Group (UK) Ltd,
Croydon CR0 4YY

Library of Congress Control Number: 2023948002

British Library Cataloguing in Publication Data

A catalogue record for this book is available from the
British Library

ISBN 978-1-5297-9530-1
ISBN 978-1-5297-9529-5 (pbk)

CONTENTS

ABOUT THE CLPE

CENTRE FOR **LITERACY**
IN PRIMARY EDUCATION

The **Centre for Literacy in Primary Education** is a UK-based children's literacy charity working with primary schools. Our work raises the achievement of children's reading and writing by helping schools to teach literacy creatively and effectively, putting quality children's books at the heart of all learning. We offer courses at our literacy library in central London and also deliver training in various regional locations.

clpe.org.uk/

About the author

Farrah Serroukh is a former primary teacher and is now the Research and Development Director at the Centre for Literacy in Primary Education (CLPE). She developed and is the author of CLPE's ground-breaking Reflecting Realities Survey of Ethnic Representation within UK Children's Literature and leads on all work relating to this research. Farrah was awarded the UKLA Brenda Eastwood Award in 2019, and also received the prestigious NATE Diversity and Inclusion Award in 2021, in recognition of her pioneering work.

FOREWORD

by Joseph Coelho (Children's Laureate 2022–4)

I was 10 years old in 1990 when Dr Rudine Sims Bishop wrote her legendary work *Mirrors, Windows, and Sliding Glass Doors* (Bishop, 1990). I have no recollection from that time of having ever seen anyone who looked or lived like me ever in a book, film or TV show. It is difficult, even for a poet, to put into words the impact that never seeing yourself reflected can have. How do you describe an absence? How do you point out a pain that has always been there? Like many children of the time my reading diet then was mainly Roald Dahl and C.S Lewis heavy. I enjoyed the stories. I could relate to Charlie's poverty and love for chocolate, but his story would never be mine. I would never be Danny the Champion of The World. I adored Narnia and was desperate to go, but I didn't have a big house and a big old wardrobe. I could enjoy these stories, sure.

I could relate to some extent to the characters and their circumstances but because I *never* saw myself in any characters ever, all stories became ones that I was simply watching, rarely participating in. It's not that a reader can't ever connect with characters different to them, of course they can, I would argue it is essential as part of a broad and diversified reading diet that they do. But when you *never* see yourself, not ever, not once, stories become a realm you are not invited into. The aspirations and wins and hopes and dreams of characters forever remain locked away because, as a reader, there has never been the invitation for you to cross the threshold, to see yourself within the pages.

The impact of this was brought home to me on watching a superhero movie. *Black Panther* was on in the cinema, and I unexpectedly welled up. I was surprised, I was a little embarrassed to be wiping my eyes at a family-friendly action movie. It dawned on me that I had never seen so many people of colour on screen at once. Seeing that reflection, that recognition was palpable. I thought back to the mostly, or entirely, white spaces I had had to navigate throughout my life. Whilst studying Archaeology at UCL, on the rare occasions I would pass another person of colour we would nod our heads in recognition despite being strangers. A silent acknowledgement of the constant background feeling of being other and othered. A recognition that despite never seeing anyone that looked like us on screen or in books going to university, we somehow still imagined that path for ourselves.

I can't fully explain what it feels like to never see yourself represented. I can only highlight aspects of the pain. But the joy that results when you do get to be part of the story is immense, it's easier and more comfortable to explain. It was in sixth form when the poet Jean Binta Breeze visited my school. She sat on our school stage and read a poem and my entire drama class were silenced into awe. I often speak about this moment as being pivotal in becoming a writer and it was, but it took many other instances as well for the path to be clearly set out. I had to see other writers like me (and some nothing like me) some with shared backgrounds but different cultures, shared challenges but different homes, shared accents but different beliefs. I needed to see myself within a broad church of writers to gain the confidence to tread the path. As a deep and complex being I needed the opportunity to see myself in the humour of Michael Rosen's poems and the lyrical dexterity of the poetry of Breis, and to learn from the wonderful educational practices of Jacob Sam La Rose and the deep thought and heart tugging urgency of Lemn Sissay's work and the determination and theatrical prowess of Francesca Beard's one-woman shows. I believe I became a poet first because that world included me right from the off. It took literal years for me to gain the same access and confidence and belief to enter into publishing and a lot of that was down to me never seeing myself in books or within bookmakers.

All this is to say that the work done here by CLPE and through that work by schools and teachers and librarians and you, is life changing and essential. It goes beyond merely allowing children to see themselves as writers or to see themselves in books, it speaks to the very nature of the society we need to create. One of empathy and understanding, where everyone can have their horizons broadened, where everyone can be given the opportunity to reach their full potential. By learning from the work contained in these pages, you're bringing that reality forth out of the realm of fiction and into reality.

ABOUT THIS BOOK

This book is the result of what happens when we ask the seemingly simple question:

Do we have ethnically inclusive and representative literature that reflects the realities of our learners and the wider world?

In asking this question of the UK publishing industry through our annual Reflecting Realities surveys, we have learnt that although their output does feature such titles, the volume of output has not been sufficient to ensure that children encounter a breadth and range of quality representations. The process has revealed a great deal about the ways in which racially minoritised characters are portrayed within children's literature, corroborating and building on the work of leading thinkers in this field. This in turn has prompted the question of, **what does it mean to reflect realities authentically, meaningfully, and effectively in children's literature?** The UK publishing industry has responded to these questions with a concerted effort to increase the volume of ethnically representative literature. Through this book we will share the findings from this series of surveys, explore what the patterns and trends indicate and unpick what we have learnt from reviewing the industry's output. In this book, we will draw on this learning to support teachers in identifying common features that constitute quality inclusive and representative literature, as well as the pitfalls of titles that fall short in this regard.

Asking the opening question of the publishing industry has generated a wealth of knowledge and inspired a great deal of activity and advocacy within and beyond the publishing sector. This has been encouraging and highlights the importance of contemplating the intention that sits beneath the question. We believe that there is a crucial value in ensuring access to quality inclusive and representative literature and as such, this should be a fundamental entitlement for all children. In the chapters that follow we will discuss the powerful ways teachers can provide affirmation, challenge thinking, and broaden outlooks through the introduction and use of representative literature.

We will also share what happens when we ask the same initial 'simple' question of the teaching profession. By asking this of 30 practitioners across 10 schools and working alongside 300 children over a three-year period, as part of a classroom-based action research project, we have learnt a great deal about how essential and transformative meaningful access to quality inclusive and representative literature can be for children's learner, reader, and writer identity.

Over the duration of the project, it has become apparent that this question is the tip of a very deep iceberg. One participating teacher for example reflected that, *'It has made me reflect on the extent of representation and inclusion beyond literacy and across our programmes of study.'* What such reflections have revealed is that beneath the iceberg tip sits a series of questions that highlight the extent of the work required to ensure meaningful inclusive practices in the primary sector. If we ask whether schools have inclusive representative literature in their stock, it becomes quickly apparent that we must then also ask:

- Do children have opportunities to access and meaningfully engage with this literature?
- Do children have the opportunity to learn directly from the writers who produce this literature and are these creators from a range of backgrounds?
- Does this literature form an integral basis of our literacy programme of study?
- Does this literature form the basis of our wider programmes of study?
- Are all our resources inclusive and do they support the study of these texts?
- Does our provision meet the needs and interests of every learner by reflecting their realities and the realities of the wider world?

Exploring how best to support schools to be more critically reflective and actively engaged in ensuring inclusive and anti-racist practices in Literacy teaching and learning, through arts-based approaches, has invited the opportunity to interrogate what is required to cultivate a positive relationship with reading and writing. By contemplating and trialling ways forward, we believe we have arrived at the key ingredients that necessitate a healthy autonomous learner identity and help shape a rich and engaging learning culture.

This book aims to distil the learning from the very first question and every question it has inspired since. We hope that it will encourage teachers, school librarians and other literacy professionals to ask the same questions of their own contexts and in doing so support you in finding answers that will help provide the best possible experience for the young learners in your care.

ACKNOWLEDGEMENTS

This book shares what we have learnt from our Reflecting Realities work. When we began to think about this work in 2016 our aim was to produce an annual survey to provide data that would support understanding about the extent and quality of ethnic representation in children's literature published in the UK. It was our hope that the learning and insights from this process would contribute to public discourse and help drive improvements in this area.

The Reflecting Realities work has developed into so much more than the production of the survey, and this book is one of those developments. All of this work combined requires an enormous amount of time, expertise and labour. It has required commitment, support and hard work from the widest range of people who have helped us to do landscape-changing work; they have provided the eco-system within which we have been able to nurture and grow Reflecting Realities, giving us the evidence and the insights that we share with you in this book.

We are indebted to Sarah Crown and Arts Council England for not only wholeheartedly embracing and believing in our vision from inception, but also funding us to be able to introduce and sustain this work; to Charlotte House and the Paul Hamlyn Foundation for their generous support, enabling us to take this work into schools in a meaningful way.

The wisdom, expertise, guidance and unwavering support of the Steering Group – Darren Chetty, Dr Fen Coles, Louise Johns-Shepherd, Professor Vini Lander, Nicky Parker, Dr Zaahida Nabagereka, Dr Melanie Ramdarshan Bold, Professor Karen Sands-O'Connor and Holly Tonks – has been truly invaluable from the beginning of this project and throughout the production of every single report.

The intern teams from University College London, Bath Spa University and City University alongside our dedicated CLPE staff team have been instrumental in meticulously reviewing every single title submitted to enable the data generation for each report.

The goodwill and continued participation of the UK children's publishing industry is key to the success of this work and demonstrates a genuine commitment to better representation in children's literature. Alongside our charity partners and others who have worked in this space for many years, we have all shown that change is possible, and the future can look different.

We do not take for granted the honesty, generosity and trust that the creatives involved in this work have given in abundance, particularly to those who have worked with us on the Reflecting Realities in the Classroom Project. The teachers and their children have benefitted in deep and profound ways and we are tremendously grateful to Valerie Bloom, Maisie Chan, Joseph Coelho, Lucy Farfort, Karl Nova, S.F. Said, Nadia Shireen, Ken Wilson-Max and Benjamin Zephaniah for enabling this.

We appreciate that being open to researching and examining your own practice can be daunting and time consuming – particularly given the immense challenges that so many face in the contemporary classroom. We have been deeply moved by the passion and commitment of the project leads, class teachers, senior leaders and wider school communities involved in this research project. We'd like to express special thanks to the class teachers and project leads for their dedication, trust and hard work; it has been an absolute honour to go on this journey with you and we would not have been able to generate the evidence we share in this book without you.

The Reflecting Realities in the Classroom Year 1 and 2 Project teachers:

- Aylea Abassi
- Jean Atkins
- Kerry Austin
- Sophie Balaam
- Naheed Bashir
- Kate Beckingham
- Jean Bennett
- Anna Bryan
- Kayla Campbell
- Natalie Caraccio
- Rosie Clemson
- Jessie Cunningham
- Lorna Dockworth
- Alex Duffy
- Scarlett Ferro
- Darren Gardiner
- Anna Garratt
- Anna Given
- Charlotte Guilmartin-Cole
- Laura Hall
- Annette Hart
- Lucy Johansson
- Bernie Keane
- Daisy Killeen
- Vicky Linke
- Edward Lockwood Wells
- Jessie Maoza
- Tara Nyarko
- Kerry O'Doherty
- Tejal Ruparelia
- Whitney Shore
- Alannah Stephenson

The Reflecting Realities in the Classroom Project schools:

- Albemarle Primary
- Chesterton Primary
- Christ Church CE Primary
- Hackbridge Primary
- Hillbrook Primary
- Paxton Primary
- Ravenstone Primary
- Regina Coeli
- Swaffield Primary
- West Ashtead Primary
- West Hill Primary

Throughout the Reflecting Realities in the Classroom Project we have benefitted from the enthusiasm and support of the Wandle Teaching School Alliance who championed the project and helped us to recruit the participating schools. We are particularly indebted to Theresa

Moses and Davina Salmon for being passionate advocates of the project and to Matthew Courtney for his invaluable attention to detail, diligence, expertise and dedication. Our evidence base is much richer and more detailed because of Matthew's work.

The response and engagement of teachers, librarians, creatives and wider stakeholders to all aspects of our Reflecting Realities work has been profoundly humbling and is testament to the collective desire for things to be better. It is this desire and the hope that fuels it that sustains our efforts and drive. It is a real privilege to stand shoulder to shoulder with an ever-growing body of people invested in improving the publishing and educational landscape to improve the bookshelves of today to help make a better tomorrow for all.

Thank you

Farrah Serroukh

Louise Johns-Shepherd

And all the staff at CLPE

IMAGE ACKNOWLEDGEMENTS

The author and publisher thank Scholastic for granting permission for the following book covers to be reproduced in this book on page 63:

Diver's Daughter: A Tudor Story
Text © Patrice Lawrence, 2019
Cover © Alette Straathof, 2019

Two Sisters: A Story of Freedom
Text © Kereen Getten, 2021
Cover by Alette Straathof © Scholastic, 2019

Windrush Child
Text © Benjamin Zephaniah, 2023
Cover by Two Dots Creative © Scholastic, 2023

My Story: Princess Sophia Duleep Singh
Text © Sufiya Ahmed, 2022
Cover © Euan Cook, 2022

My Story: Noor-un-Nissa Inayat Khan
Text © Sufiya Ahmed, 2020
Cover © Euan Cook, 2020

Torn Apart - The Partition of India, 1947
Text © Swapna Haddow, 2021
Cover by Two Dots Creative © Scholastic, 2021

CHAPTER 1

UNDERSTANDING THE NEED AND RATIONALE FOR REFLECTING REALITIES

> Reflecting realities means not only telling stories that reflect the truth of the world we live in now, stories that allow everyone to be and feel seen, but also telling stories that allow people to imagine and envision the possibilities of a reality where they can be whatever they want to be. I've heard it said that it's significantly harder to be what you don't see, examples of yourself when looking out at the world. This was very true of my own childhood, so if I can create the kind of work that makes it easier for others to connect those dots then I've done my job well.
>
> Dapo Adeola

Dapo Adeola is an illustrator, author and character designer who was awarded Illustrator of the Year at the British Book Awards in 2022. He is the illustrator and co-creator with the author Nathan Byron of the Rocket series which began with the widely acclaimed *Look Up!* in 2019. Dapo illustrated *My Dad is a Grizzly Bear* and *My Mum is a Lioness* written by award-winning author Swapna Haddow (both published by Macmillan Children's Books), and collaborated with Malorie Blackman on their picture book *We're Going to Find the Monster!* Dapo made his author debut in 2021 with the Puffin-published picture book *Hey You!: An Empowering Celebration of Growing Up Black*, featuring 18 talented Black British illustrators, which also went on to win Illustrated book of the year at the British Book Awards in 2022. He edited *Joyful, Joyful: Stories Celebrating Black Voices* which showcased 40 talented Black writers and artists from across the world. Born in Britain and of Nigerian heritage, Dapo is an avid believer in the importance of equal representation in the creative arts.

The quote here is from Dapo's blog 'Reflecting Realities', written for CLPE in 2020.

Find out more:

WHAT IS CLPE AND WHAT DOES IT DO?

The Centre for Literacy in Primary Education (CLPE) is a UK charity dedicated to improving the teaching of literacy in primary schools. The charity has been in existence since 1972 and has a national and international reputation for the quality of its work and research. CLPE is based in London, England, in a building which houses a library of 25,000 carefully chosen, in-print children's books; the charity provides training and teaching resources for primary schools to help them teach literacy creatively and effectively. CLPE works face-to-face with around 5,000 teachers each year and tens of thousands more teachers use the online resources to support the teaching of literacy. All the work at CLPE is designed to support teachers' knowledge about children's literature, its creators and how to use it in classrooms.

At CLPE we believe that the use of high-quality books as the foundation of an English curriculum is at the very heart of a school's successful approach to engaging and supporting children to become motivated and independent readers. We outlined our approach to putting the very best books at the centre of literacy learning in our previous book *The Power of a Rich Reading Curriculum* (CLPE, 2020b) and in this book, we touched upon the importance and interrelated nature of reading and writing and how a child's sense of learner identity can impact on their ability to progress and succeed in all areas of literacy. We also spoke about the importance of curating a book stock that truly reflected the realities of the classroom and the world within which children live. This is an underpinning principle for all our work at CLPE and needs to be a principle for anyone who is building a classroom or school library.

Since 2016 we've been working on evidencing this principle, on developing our thinking and on supporting teachers to put this principle into practice. In this book you'll see how starting with the learner and meaningfully developing the reading and the writing identity of all learners really can improve literacy teaching in classrooms.

WHAT IS THE REFLECTING REALITIES SURVEY AND WHY DO CLPE PUBLISH IT EVERY YEAR?

At CLPE we identify areas of research that we feel will resonate and be relevant to the needs and interests of our profession, as well as the needs of the child learner. Ensuring that classroom bookshelves are stocked with high-quality representative and inclusive literature has always been important. Within the context of the world in which they are produced, books not only serve as means to support children in their journey towards literacy but they also have the scope to serve as vehicles of social justice.

The challenge of sourcing representative literature is something we and others have been working on for many years and we knew that in the work of curating booklists, course texts and library stock at CLPE it was often a real struggle to find enough books to offer real choice and range to the schools we work with. If we, with our access to the publishing industry and their output, were struggling to curate broad, varied, inclusive and representative book collections then how could we insist that this standard be adhered to in classrooms around the country?

From experience we knew that this had been a longstanding issue and that there had been a great deal of advocacy over many years in this area by parents, librarians, creatives, independent publishers, book sellers and community groups. However, we also knew that there had never been a comprehensive study of the extent of the issue within the UK. In the US, the Cooperative Children's Book Centre at the University of Madison Wisconsin School of Education has been producing an annual survey that reports on the number of characters of colour and authors of colour in children's literature produced in the US for over three decades (ccbc.education.wisc.edu/literature-resources/ccbc-diversity-statistics/). The UK did not have an equivalent study.

In 2016, with this in mind, we began seeking funding to produce an annual survey that would give us an insight into the extent and quality of representation of racially minoritised characters. Once funding was secured, we met and spoke with representatives from across UK publishing houses, large and small, to explain our intention, the aims of the work and to encourage them to participate. We devised an analysis framework that would enable us to review each title to determine the extent and quality of this presence. The first report was published in 2018 and, since then, it has become an annual report. By offering quantitative and qualitative data, it was our hope that we would help contribute to more nuanced reflections in this area. This would allow us to disrupt the supply and demand chain by holding the industry to account, encouraging them to do better and providing the tools to encourage teachers and librarians to be more critically reflective and demand better. The Reflecting Realities surveys, which can be freely accessed on our website at clpe.org.uk/research/reflecting-realities, provide a comprehensive annual survey of ethnic representation within UK children's literature. This survey provides important data for all stakeholders to inform a more considered conversation and help us all ensure that published children's literature meaningfully reflects the realities of its readership.

WHAT HAS REFLECTING REALITIES TAUGHT US?

The key focus from the very beginning of the Reflecting Realities work was to determine the extent and quality of the presence of racially minoritised demographic groups in UK children's literature. And this has continued to be the fundamental focus of enquiry with every survey since. The data collated from the books reviewed for that first report indicated that the extent of presence was very low and the quality was significantly lacking. It provided a benchmark against which to measure progress, progress that we were hopeful could be achieved with a collective investment of time, money and focus.

In the 2022 report we found that 5,383 children's picturebooks, fiction and non-fiction titles, eligible for the consideration of this study were published in the UK in 2021. Of these 1,059 featured characters of colour – 20 per cent, compared to 15 per cent in 2020, 10 per cent in 2019, 7 per cent in 2018 and 4 per cent in 2017.

EXTENT OF PRESENCE OF CHARACTERS OF COLOUR IN CHILDREN'S LITERATURE PUBLISHED IN THE UK OVER FIVE-YEAR PERIOD

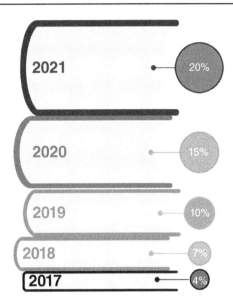

Figure 1.1   Percentage of Children's Books published featuring Racially Minoritised Characters (Reflecting Realities Survey 2021) ©CLPE 2022/2023

The first report was published at a point in time when the public discourse regarding the need for better inclusion was prompting much introspection across industries. We could not have anticipated just how responsive the publishing industry would be. There is no doubt that the continuous upward trend we have observed with each survey has transformed the volume of representative and inclusive literature available to young readers in the UK during this short time. We have learnt that, when intentions are set, investments are made and time is dedicated to an end, remarkable feats can be achieved, as borne out by the trajectory of the summary data contained within the 2022 report.

The continued positive trend in the volume of production of inclusive and representative literature shows a sustained commitment to improvement. The commendable 16 percentage point rise from the first report indicates that there are more representative titles available to young readers. This is naturally something we are very pleased to have been able to report and it is an improvement that we hope will continue to grow over time.

Increased volume alleviates the burden of one book having to shoulder the responsibility of being everything for everyone. It gives space and licence to the writer to take their chosen direction in terms of casting, characterisation, subject and themes. The weight of knowing that your book won't be the only title on the shelf featuring a character from a specific demographic group invites the opportunity to shape the character in a way that is unique to the world of their story, because you know that they will be one of many characters from this background that readers will meet. With each new encounter, readers will have the opportunity to either experience affirmation, connection or insights that help form layered impressions over time.

As we have maintained from the outset of this work, the two key indicators that inform the value of representation are volume and quality. No one demographic group is a monolith. Every individual is unique and the opportunity for readers to encounter many characters from a range of backgrounds, portrayed in a variety of ways and exploring a breadth of themes allows the contents of the average bookshelf to reflect these realities. This ideal, however, is not necessarily realised solely by an increase in output. More is not always indicative of better, and the value of increased volume can be undermined if the quality of content falls short.

In our analysis of the submissions for the reports we have found that the quality of portrayals of characters from racially minoritised backgrounds varies across and within publishing houses. In all the review cycles, we have enjoyed titles in which the quality is exemplary. However, in other instances we have encountered titles in which the portrayals required more consideration, deeper development and better refinement. What the titles that do it well suggest is that the knowledge, skill and creative capacity to produce quality representative literature exists. No doubt it always did. The momentum of recent years seems to have encouraged a collective growth of activity. It's important that this energy continues and that it is directed towards developing understanding of what works and applying this knowledge with consistency across the publishing industry, making this knowledge central to the creative process.

REFLECTING REALITIES IN THE CLASSROOM: THE NEXT STEP

As mentioned, the Reflecting Realities reports are all available to download for free from the CLPE website and many teachers have found them extremely helpful to support their work in schools. However, the survey and the publications were designed to provide statistics and qualitative insights into the output of the publishing industry and, while we had hoped that they would be useful to teachers in schools, they weren't necessarily designed with teachers as the primary audience.

We had always envisaged that these reports would be the first part of a much longer piece of work. Scrutinising publishing output is the necessary first step which we hoped would trigger a chain reaction that would result in long-term sustainable change for child readers.

CLPE MODEL OF CHANGE TO SUPPORT BETTER VOLUME AND QUALITY OF ETHNICALLY REPRESENTATIVE BOOK STOCK IN SCHOOLS THAT REFLECT THE REALITIES OF THE SCHOOL AND WIDER COMMUNITY

A crucial part of the next phase of this mission as outlined in Figure 1.2 would necessitate supporting teachers to critically reflect on publishing output and its use within the education sector, and show how book stock curation has an effect, and can affect our work in classrooms. We hoped that this in turn would lead to greater discernment and encourage more demand for good-quality representative literature which would sustain publishers' motivation to continue to work hard to meet this demand. We are keen that through the implementation of this model of change we can help to reduce the risk of the positive uplift established during this period becoming a momentary trend that diminishes over time. Instead, we want this cyclical process to enable a permanent shift that ensures a continuous supply of high-quality inclusive titles for young readers. To this end, the CLPE has run a range of training for school staff, helping them to use the reports, the language, the questions and the examples of good practice within them which has encouraged considerable interest in the work across the educational landscape.

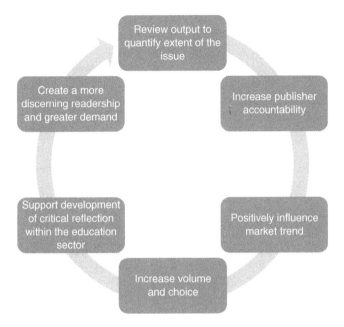

Figure 1.2   Model of Change to support better Production and Critical Engagement of Ethnically Representative Literature for Children ©CLPE 2022/2023

In our wider work, we have seen the enormous impact of inclusive literacy practice on reading and writing outcomes across the primary age range. The negative impact of a literary space where children do not see themselves has been well documented; we hear anecdotal accounts of exclusion all the time. We also hear stories of inspiration about the powerful impact of properly inclusive learning environments where children see themselves in the texts they study and are able to develop strong and positive senses of themselves as readers and writers.

At the beginning of the 2021 school year, we began a classroom-based, action research project working with ten schools in London and the Southeast of England. We aimed to track the learning journey of 300 children, over three years from Year 3 to Year 5, and to consider how providing access to quality ethnically inclusive and representative literature and working alongside British authors of colour might influence and shape children's reader and writer identity.

We have learnt so much from these schools, the teachers and the creatives who worked with us, and from the children in the classrooms. We have been able to use what we learnt in the first year of the project to support us to write this book. The quotes that you will see throughout the book are from the teachers who have been part of the project and are based on the work they have done. These, along with interviews, reflective journals and examples of work from the children in their classes, provide us with rich evidence about the importance and impact of good-quality, inclusive and creative literary experiences. We are building a significant evidence base to support our thinking and to show just how important inclusive practice is to attainment, achievement and enjoyment in literacy.

The process that the teachers have been through involved reviewing their book stock by referencing and building on the guidelines offered through our Reflecting Realities reports. Inviting them to consider how effectively their stock reflected the realities of their school community and that of wider society encouraged them to ask a series of questions that helped them to delve deeply into all aspects of their practice and provision. Interrogating the content of the book corners prompted reviews of their literacy and wider programmes of study. This in turn encouraged consideration about how they taught reading and writing and whether their approaches were inclusive and meaningful for all learners.

Their commitment to this process resulted in many teachers reporting that they were learning about aspects of their children that they had never known before, with children being more open and excitedly drawing parallels between the representative story worlds they were encountering and their own lives. Teachers were witnessing the emergence of a newfound confidence in many of their children, who seemed more keen and able to express themselves verbally and through their writing. Several teachers reported that their children's personalities and creativity began to shine through in their work, resulting in thoughtful, entertaining writing that was a pleasure to read. So, what started with the book corner ended with a thriving inclusive learning culture that inspired and empowered children to express themselves creatively.

REFLECTING REALITIES: SHAPING READER AND WRITER IDENTITY

As we said at the beginning of this chapter, our work at CLPE has always been about helping teachers improve their practice and we have always done that by considering the learner at the front and centre of any work we do. To meet the needs of a child, we need to be aware of their context, their heritage, their background, their culture, their linguistic capacities, their preferences, their needs and their interests. This knowledge helps to build an understanding of the person they are and enables us to meet them where we find them. All of these elements will inform and shape their learner, reader and writer identity.

To become real readers, children need to develop their reader identity. They need stories, poems and information books which put them and their world on the bookshelf and that do so in a way that validates them as a reader and a learner. They need the time, space and opportunity to discover their preferences and their passions and they need skilled, trained adults who can guide them towards texts, teach them the skills to decode the text, make sense of the construction and respond to the experience.

In chapters 3 and 4, we look at how what children experience in the literacy classroom shapes their learner identity and then their reader identity. We will explore a range of questions including: what do we know about our children? How do we find out? How do we use this knowledge to shape a learning experience, community and culture that enables every child to thrive? And then, what role do books and our reading culture play in this aspect of our work?

In chapter 5, we will consider: what does an inclusive classroom look like? How do we create the best opportunities for learning? How do we build on the knowledge of the learner? And we will offer plenty of practical suggestions for reviewing your provision and practice, and support you in planning ways to develop reader identity.

We have learnt a lot about why representation in texts is important in terms of developing reader identity and we will share with you some of the key considerations in choosing and using texts. We will consider how our text choices help to shape our book corners and how these choices shape a child's reading journey, classroom practice and the reading culture – and why this is important.

Our work at CLPE is built on the importance of the interrelated nature of reading and writing as set out in one of our most influential publications, *The Reader in the Writer* (Barrs and Cork, 2001). Chapter 6 and 7 look at how writer identity builds on and from reader identity. These chapters also show the importance of creative professionals as role models in demystifying the process and inspiring budding writers and outline the process of empowering children to find their voice as writers.

We look at what an authentic writing process looks like, how we can support children to develop an appreciation and understanding of the craft of writing, build an awareness of audience and how this can support children to develop autonomy and creativity in their writing.

Through this work we have focused on considering inclusivity specifically from a racial perspective as this has been the core focus of our Reflecting Realities work. We are pleased to see that our work has invited wider considerations about other protected characteristics and encouraged efforts to challenge and seek improvement in these areas of output and provision. We hope that this book will help you to understand the importance of a truly inclusive classroom and give you practical ways forward to support the children in your classroom.

We began this work because we wanted to change the book corners in the schools we work in and the reading experiences for the children we work with. Learning to read is a social process and it is intensely linked with self-image. Put simply, the reading experience can be compromised if we never come across a character or story that reflects our life, culture or background. We also know so much now about how important reading is to developing empathy and broadening outlook; ensuring an opportunity for all children to come across reading material that reflects the wider world in which they live has never been more important.

We know that this work sits within a wider societal context. To achieve what we set out to do requires deep and systemic change. We don't presume to think that we can do this alone, and we don't think that we would achieve anything if we did. We know our aim is shared by many others who are all working towards a similar aim and we celebrate the many partnerships this work has enabled us to make, not least with those schools and teachers who have taken a leap with us and joined us on this journey. We hope that their experience and our work is helpful to you as you too embark on this important road.

CHAPTER 2

FOSTERING AN INCLUSIVE LEARNING CULTURE TO HELP NURTURE LEARNER IDENTITY

Consider how reflect has more than one meaning.

Our reality in the UK includes diversity. Even if you live in a small rural village and may not see any black, or brown people – the UK, and world at large, is a big bustling place. When we come together to acknowledge and celebrate our differences, we also discover our human similarities. Through this we become stronger – more reflective.

If you don't see yourself reflected in a mirror, as a child for example, then you begin to doubt your existence. You might think you don't matter, or that you have nothing of value to say. If you don't see, or can't find, your reality reflected in the everyday things around you – the world you see, the TV, books, music, games you take pleasure in ... Then you go inward and parts of you fade away.

E.L. Norry

Emma Norry is an author who writes fiction and non-fiction for children. She is passionate about equal representation and diversity. Her first book, *Son of the Circus* (Scholastic, 2019), is part of a series that shows readers that Black and brown people have always been a part of British history. Emma has also written *Amber Undercover* (OUP, 2021) – a fun action-adventure spy story for ages ten+ and is the author of *Fablehouse* (Bloomsbury, 2023), a middle-grade fantasy series. She has many short stories in anthologies: *Happy Here* (Knights Of, 2021), *The Place for Me: Stories from the Windrush* (Scholastic, 2020) and *The Very Merry Murder Club* (Farshore, 2021). Emma's non-fiction includes biographies of Lionel Messi (Scholastic, 2020) and Nelson Mandela (Puffin, 2020).

The quote here is from Emma's blog 'Reflecting Realities', written for CLPE in 2020

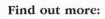 **Find out more:**

In this chapter we will dedicate time to thinking about the value of really seeing and under-standing the children that we serve. We will consider what this act of service involves and explore the fundamental importance of being open and responsive to the needs and inter-ests of every child in our care. We will also reflect on the role of literature in supporting us in achieving these aims.

To help frame your considerations, take a moment to think back on your own schooling experience. Do you recall what it felt like to be a schoolchild, not a child but a schoolchild? Were the school gates a welcome sight or a daunting prospect? What parts of school life appealed and what aspects could you have done without? What areas of learning were you drawn to and why? Were you supported to channel and develop the enthusiasm, curiosity and resilience necessary to sustain you on your learning journey? Being a schoolchild forms a core facet of our identity in the formative phase of our lives. How we perceive this aspect of our selves and how we are perceived in this regard can be instrumental to how we evolve as a learner. Take a moment to close your eyes and picture the schoolchild you once were. As the teacher you are now, how would you plan to meet the needs of the schoolchild in your mind's eye?

Those distant memories might have brought a wide range of recollections to the surface. Each of us will have had a unique experience of the schooling system. These formative experiences will have influenced the way we viewed ourselves, our peers and the world around us. We may not necessarily remember much of what we were taught but we are likely to recall how we felt at key moments and through key periods. How we interpret the world around us and view our place in it during this developmental phase has the potential to be character defining and strongly influence our academic and life trajectory.

This is why, before we pull out the lever arch files, programmes of study, textbooks, assessment trackers and the plethora of materials and tools designed to help us teach, we must start with the child. Our first and most fundamental responsibility as teachers is to see who we serve. The adult/child dynamic of the teacher/schoolchild relationship often dispro-portionately leverages the power in the teacher's favour. As educators it is important to counteract this imbalance by actively seeking to empower (Friere, 1996) children to grow into confident, knowledgeable, skilled, resilient, well-adjusted, happy individuals. Every child who passes the threshold of our classroom is a unique individual, with their own dis-tinctive perspective and a wealth of lived experience that contributes to their sense of self and understanding of the wider world. In seeking to serve them, we must meet them where they are at and tailor the teaching to best support them along their learning journey. This will involve having a sound knowledge of their needs and interests and being responsive through the planning, preparation, design and facilitation of the learning experiences we create.

Before we can begin to consider how to go about tailoring learning in this way, it is important to take the time to consider how well we know our children. We understand we need to know about attainment levels, progress points and national data benchmarks but what do we know about them as individuals? What do we know about their home lives, their families, their backgrounds and their histories? How do we find out? What mechanisms, routines and protocols are in place, at each stage of their time with us, to capture, develop and refine our understanding of each child? How do we use this knowledge to shape our teaching practices and cultivate a rich learning community and culture that enables every child to thrive? The answers to these questions are key to laying the foundations for ensuring that our practice and provision is genuinely and meaningfully inclusive.

INCLUSIVITY IN OUR LEARNING SPACES

Now, we want to think about inclusivity and what it means in our learning spaces. Take a moment to imagine yourself walking into your current school for the first time. If you like, take this exercise a step further and imagine yourself as the child you once were stepping into your current school for the first time. As you enter the space, passing signs and displays in communal areas, what does the content suggest to you about the values and culture of this place? What's important? What matters? Who matters? How do you know? Are the identities, experiences and cultures of every child recognised and present in these spaces? Do they offer insights into communities and worlds beyond their own? Do they form a meaningful part of the aesthetic or are the walls covered in generic posters featuring hollow slogans that in their attempt to have universal appeal, fail to have any real relevance at all other than to serve as wallpaper?

As you tune into the hum of conversation that ripples through the corridors and echoes from classroom doorways, what do you hear? Do children feel comfortable enough and are they given the space to express all aspects of themselves? Do they feel confident in sharing insights into their everyday lives, their likes and dislikes, their fascinations, as well as their linguistic, cultural and familial heritage without fear of judgement? Are they supported to share their opinions, to think out loud and evolve their thinking? Are they encouraged to listen respectfully while their peers share their thoughts and ideas, and do they have the sensitivity and skills to exchange ideas and differences of opinion in a healthy and constructive way that elevates the learning for all? When we take the time to really listen to what children have to say, their words or, indeed, their lack of words tell us so much about what sits beneath the surface.

Schools are institutions designed to lay the groundwork for socialising children to become part of society at large. Every child will negotiate a way of being within this system that works for them. In the quest to fit in, sadly, many will learn very early on to mask or suppress parts of themselves. Many will internalise explicit and implicit messages about the 'right' way to be and present a version of themselves based on how they perceive the messages conveyed in the school space. To feel truly included a child must feel confident to bring their whole self to school without parking key parts of their identity at the classroom door – a principle that was explicitly encouraged as far back as the 1975 Bullock Report: *No child should be expected to cast off the language and culture of the home as he crosses the school threshold, nor to live and act as though school and home represent two totally separate and different cultures which have to be kept firmly apart* (DfE, 1975).

To thrive, they must experience learning opportunities that are tailored to their needs and interests, support them in making personal connections, build their knowledge and skills base, challenge their thinking and broaden their outlook. This means we must carefully consider the design and content of our programmes of study. As you continue to imagine yourself walking through the classrooms of your school, think about what and who the children are learning about. Who and what determines this? How do teachers decide? How much agency and opportunity do children have to make choices about what and how they learn? Do teachers tap into the pool of every child's personal experience, interests and linguistic and cultural backgrounds to build, shape and enrich the learning? Do the programmes of study and learning culture enable children to feel seen and heard? Are they empowered to take risks? Do they feel like valued contributors to the construction of ideas and collective evolution of their learning community?

As you glance at the resource stations, the trays and shelves, what do the materials indicate about how much consideration has been given to ensuring that these are inclusive both in terms of accessibility and in terms of relatability? Are home corners and role play areas brimming with a breadth of representations of real-life packaging, as well as foods and utensils found across a range of cultures? Do the art materials allow scope for selecting and mixing palettes that depict the whole spectrum of skin tones and complexions? Do the displays offer scope for affirming the lives of young learners, valuing their contributions, while also building their knowledge and broadening their outlook?

Finally, turn your attention to the bookshelves. What kinds of books are available to the children? Are there a breadth and range of text types, covering a range of topics and themes and set across a variation of eras, places and communities? Do the casts of characters and communities depicted reflect the realities, facets of identities and cultures of the children and offer insights into worlds beyond their own? Do children have the opportunity to meaningfully engage with these titles? How are these books integrated into the core literacy programme of study and wider curriculum areas?

> *It's not just about swapping out a few books across your curriculum with a few more that feature characters of colour on the front covers. It's so much deeper than that.*
>
> **Senior leader**

Through this imaginary tour of your school, what conclusions have you drawn about the extent of its inclusivity? Are you pleasantly surprised or is there work to be done? We all know that the job of a teacher is never truly done. Every day, every child in every moment challenges our thinking, encourages us to adapt, to be creative and enables us to grow as a teacher. It is this uncertainty, tension and challenge that can be both scary and thrilling but also makes the job the interesting, inspiring and rewarding vocation that it is.

The scarcity of time and the intensity of the load of our labour can mean that we rarely have the opportunity to pause for thought about the significance of our impact on the learners in our care and our aspirations for their growth. What is your hope for the children that you teach? On a day-to-day basis how do you hope they will feel about themselves as individuals and as learners? How do you hope they will perceive and engage with their learning community? When they leave the school gates, what are the key things you hope they will have internalised so that they can navigate the world beyond their school community?

The preservation of hope is a key component of nurturing the next generation. But hope alone will not suffice. It is imperative that this hopefulness is married with thoughtfully considered and consistently good inclusive practice. So, in that vein, consider how your responses to these questions correspond to what you do and how you do it as a teacher. How do these aspirations inform and shape your practice and provision? What does the term 'inclusive practice' mean to you and how does it manifest in your day-to-day practice?

REFLECTIVE PRACTICE TO SUPPORT THE DEVELOPMENT OF AN INCLUSIVE LEARNING CULTURE

Reflective practice is at the core of what makes a good teacher. Questioning what we want children to gain from their learning experiences – within and beyond books – is the first step. Considerations around how to create a learning culture that gives licence to all children to be should be at the core of this reflective practice. This principle relates as much to the teaching of writing as anything else. The writing output along with children's reflections provide tangible evidence of children's competency and perspective. This in turn enables us to consider how we might support them to move forward in evolving their authorial voice and build story worlds that draw from their experiences and reflect their interests and fascinations.

Giving children the permission or licence to be themselves involves an ongoing series of key steps of reflective practice as outlined in Figure 2.1. We must start with a baseline consciousness of how and to what extent we create a space in which every child feels like a valued member of the class community, able to share their thoughts, feelings and perspective and contribute to all aspects of school life. Through our planning and preparation, we must ask: how do we ensure that we provide materials and resources that anticipate and respond to children's interests? How do the resources channel the experiences and perspectives of each child? A simple example of this as referenced previously might be the extent to which the kitchen in an Early Years role play area contains packaging, foodstuffs and utensils that the

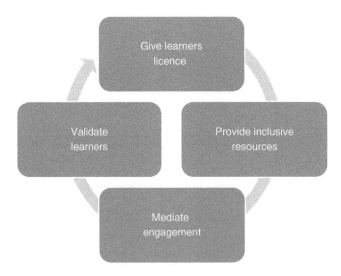

Figure 2.1   Cycle of Key Practices to Support the Development of an Inclusive Learning Culture ©CLPE 2022/2023

children will identify with. We must then consider whether every child has the opportunity to express themselves both through facilitated one-to-one dialogue, group and whole-class discussions as well as carefully planned learning experiences. It is important to then determine whether the learning we plan helps to affirm and validate each child. If we routinely ask these questions of ourselves and sustain these steps, this will lead to a cycle of validation that gives children the opportunity, confidence and licence to be themselves in the learning space.

EVALUATING INCLUSIVE PRACTICES

Take a moment to consider this cycle within the context of your own setting and create a table such as the one shown in Figure 2.2 to note the ways in which you currently adopt these practices.

This last exercise may have raised more questions than answers. Affirming and valuing a child in the learning space requires a multi-layered approach and sustained effort that will require adaptation over time. There is not an end point at which this work is done because children are humans in the formative phase of their lives who will need different kinds of affirmation at different stages of their development which will depend on a whole host of factors.

	Approaches, routines or practices that have worked well …
Giving learners licence How do I create a space in which every child feels like a valued member of my class community, able to share their thoughts, feelings and perspective and contribute to all aspects of school life?	
Providing inclusive resources How do I ensure that the learning environment is resourced with materials that meaningfully recognise facets of children's identities, heritage and culture? How do I use resources to anticipate and respond to children's interests? How do I ensure that the resources channel the experiences and perspectives of each child?	
Mediating engagement How do I ensure that every child has the opportunity to express themselves both through facilitated one-to-one, group and whole-class discussions as well as carefully planned learning experiences?	
Validating learners How does the learning space and planned experiences help to affirm and validate each child?	

Figure 2.2   Guide to Support Evaluation of Key Inclusive Practices ©CLPE 2022/2023

AFFIRMING PRACTICES IN THE CLASSROOM

This is why really getting to know our children and understanding their needs and interests is so crucial to enabling us to do the best job we can do. One way to support the embedding of this cycle of reflective practice is to unpick further how to map elements of teaching practice and provision to the idea of having the licence to be. As outlined in Figure 2.3, the licence to be ourselves in the learning space requires us to adopt a broad range of affirming practices. Let's take each of these affirming practices and consider them in a little more detail.

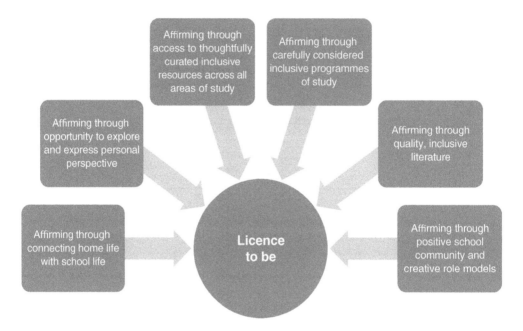

Figure 2.3   Key Classroom Practices to Affirm Learners' Licence to Be ©CLPE 2022/2023

AFFIRMING THROUGH CONNECTING HOME LIFE WITH SCHOOL LIFE

Children come to school with their very own unique outlook that has been informed and shaped by their lived experiences. Making sense of new information will involve drawing on what they already know and believe to support their thinking. The process of teaching involves helping children to make connections to enable understanding, challenge thinking and build their knowledge base. Testing ideas and challenging thinking involve trial and error which is core to any learning process. The making of mistakes and the necessity of sitting with uncertainty that learning new things involves requires a level of vulnerability. Sharing knowledge drawn from elements of your personal life can require an even deeper level of vulnerability, particularly if you feel that this may not be welcomed. This is why it is imperative to foster strong home–school links.

We've had a couple of coffee mornings for the parents. We've used these to open up conversations with them about this work. We got them to think about what their favourite stories were when they were growing up, including stories shared orally. We talked about how important it is for them to share these stories with their children. From these conversations, I think there seems to be a sense of there being distinctions between what is and isn't appropriate to share in terms of culture. So, for our families that were not born here, I think they feel that their children are coming to school to learn English and that they've kind of almost shut the door on sharing their cultural richness in this space.

Senior leader

These links provide us with much needed wider context to support our understanding of each child and help us to be able to support children in making those all-important connections as part of the learning process. It is also important in terms of building a child's self-esteem and can shift the dynamic of the child–teacher relationship from a passive model, in which the child is an empty vessel waiting to be filled with knowledge from the all-knowing fountain of knowledge that is the teacher, to a co-constructive model, in which all parties recognise that the classroom is a learning space and that as invested learners we all work collaboratively as teachers and children to co-construct meaning, acquire knowledge and skills and make sense of our world by pooling our collective insights and efforts. The latter model makes for a much richer, more vibrant and authentic learning community in which everyone feels valued and empowered.

FOSTERING STRONG HOME-SCHOOL CONNECTIONS

There are many ways in which you can create opportunities to foster and grow strong connections between home and school. Some examples:

- home/school visits
- parent story times
- show and tell
- creating memory boxes
- integration of bilingual resources
- planning topics that allow opportunity to draw on personal interests.

TAKE TIME TO CONSIDER

How will you create opportunities to foster strong home–school connections?

AFFIRMING THROUGH OPPORTUNITY TO EXPLORE AND EXPRESS PERSONAL PERSPECTIVES

If the foundation of our learning culture is grounded in the understanding that we are a learning community in which each individual is a valued member and contributor in the quest for knowledge, this will make for a healthy dynamic that encourages openness, risk-taking and sharing. To create space for this dynamic in a way that enables children to engage with confidence, the community ethos must be underpinned by kindness, sensitivity, trust and respect. These core elements will encourage children to feel that their perspective matters, is valued and will be respectfully received. Creating varied opportunities and mediums to express personal perspectives is important as some children will be more confident sharing in more intimate groupings, while others might prefer to express themselves in writing or through art or music. It is also important to recognise that like adults some children may not want to necessarily share personal perspectives at times and so this must also be respected. The point is not that all children at all times should be required to express their personal perspective but instead they should feel safe, respected and valued enough to know that they can should they wish to.

> *I think that the children have the freedom now, they feel able to create somebody that is more representative of them. Using authentic names, using authentic colours. And I think they also just feel more confident talking about themselves and talking about things that are happening at home.*

> *And they demand it now, if there's a particular celebration or a special day for them at home or something that's going on in their religion or in their heritage, a lot of them now will feel confident coming into school and saying, 'Oh, Ms F, this is what's happening. Can we talk about it? Can I do a presentation on it? Can I share this with my friends and family or share this with my friends at school?' I think that's something that's quite new because I don't think they felt able to do that before.*

Class teacher

OPPORTUNITIES TO EXPLORE AND EXPRESS PERSONAL PERSPECTIVES

Classrooms can be safe spaces for children to share and explore their authentic selves. Class teachers can find ways to shape an environment that welcomes and champions this, and create opportunities for children to make this real. Some examples:

- establishing clear protocols for respectful listening
- maintaining role play areas and props across key stages
- providing children with writing journals to note thoughts, feelings and ideas
- creating a communication box for children to post letters to you
- allowing time to respond to poetry
- home/school visits
- parent story times

- show and tell
- creating memory boxes
- integration of bilingual resources
- planning topics that allow opportunity to draw on personal interests.

TAKE TiME TO CONSiDER

How do I create opportunities for children to explore and express personal perspectives?

AFFiRMiNG THROUGH ACCESS TO THOUGHTFULLY CURATED INCLUSiVE RESOURCES ACROSS ALL AREAS OF STUDY

We dedicate a significant amount of time to planning and preparing our lessons. We also carefully consider how to resource them in a way that will support and enhance the learning. Another component to these considerations should involve determining how inclusive the materials and resources we use are. If, for example, the children are participating in an art lesson that requires them to create depictions of people, then do they have access to art materials that will enable them to create a range of skin tones and complexions? Have the children been taught the skill of colour mixing to enable them to generate the skin tones that they wish to create? Affirming practices can be both explicitly and implicitly expressed. The content of our lessons and facilitation of them will offer scope to explicitly affirm children based on the extent to which this content is inclusive. The resources we make available function on an implicit level in that they have the scope to undermine or consolidate the sense of affirmation our learners might feel depending on the extent of their inclusivity. The two must work hand in hand.

Think about how your learning displays reflect the ethnic, linguistic and cultural backgrounds of your children. Consider how the resources for each lesson enable children to express their own perspectives.

TAKE TiME TO CONSiDER

How do I ensure that the learning space and my lessons are resourced with inclusive materials?

AFFiRMiNG THROUGH CAREFULLY CONSiDERED INCLUSiVE PROGRAMMES OF STUDY

What does the content of our programmes of study across subject areas convey about what and who is worthy of study? The 2014 curriculum outlines overarching expectations in terms of principles and key content in each subject, but there is a great deal of scope to exercise our professional judgement to determine how we tailor content on a granular level to meet the needs and interests of our children. If we are to nurture the global citizens of tomorrow, we have a duty to ensure that they learn about the inter-relationship between people, communities, regions, societies and nations. It is important that they appreciate how artistic, linguistic, cultural, sociological, ideological and scientific developments across space and time have influenced thinking. It is crucial that they understand how the past has shaped the lives we live today and, ultimately, it is paramount that they see the interconnectedness of humanity. With this in mind, we should consider what opportunities are available for children to encounter public figures from a range of backgrounds and walks of life across all disciplines. They should experience a range of communities and cultures that help to broaden their outlook. They should engage with a breadth of schools of thought, beliefs, spiritual practices, ideological perspectives and political movements over time to better understand the different ways in which we make sense of the world and the ways in which we seek to be a part of it. There should be a progression in the content, subject matter and critical thinking required to engage with the learning within and across year groups so that by the time our children leave us in Year 6 they have a strong sense of self-worth, a breadth of knowledge about the world beyond their doorstep and the critical skills to process new information in an intelligent and balanced way.

Think about your existing foundation subject programmes of study. How broad and balanced is the coverage? Consider how you might work with colleagues within and across key stages to plan your foundation subject topics to ensure a breadth and balance of coverage. Consider whether your book stock reflects and complements this breadth.

TAKE TiME TO CONSiDER

How do I ensure that my programmes of study are inclusive?

AFFIRMiNG THROUGH QUALITY, iNCLUSIVE LiTERATURE

Throughout this book, we will speak at length about the value of accessing and meaningfully engaging with inclusive literature. Each affirming facet detailed in the graphic in Figure 2.3 holds a mirror up to the learner, enabling them to feel seen and valued within the learning space. The sense of belonging this instils can support a child in developing the confidence and inclination to be themselves and bring themselves more fully into the learning space. The scope for connection afforded by representative and inclusive books makes this particular facet instrumental to this work. Quality literature is a key component of our provision and, when complemented with affirming and carefully considered creative teaching practices, it can support us in cultivating a rich learning community and culture.

Do your children have the opportunity to choose new books for the classroom? How regularly do you review your classroom stock? When text mapping for your literacy programme of study do you consider the breadth and balance of representative titles featured?

TAKE TiME TO CONSiDER

How do I ensure that the books available to my children are inclusive?

AFFiRMiNG THROUGH POSiTiVE SCHOOL, COMMUNiTY AND CREATiVE ROLE MODELS

The people who make up our school, local and wider community serve as important role models for our children. Through their example, children are offered a window into the future of possibilities of who, what and how they might be. Many of us will have practices in our settings that channel these role model resources such as delivering a 'people in our community' project, organising a reading volunteer programme or arranging class visits to local community projects. It is worth considering how we extend this principle within our literacy programmes of study by utilising authors, poets and illustrators. The value of learning first-hand about an author's creative process can be illuminating for children who are in the formative phase of developing their own relationship with writing.

> *Some of our young Black boys now play 'Karl Nova' and 'Joseph Coelho' in the playground. They see themselves in these creatives and now describe themselves as poets.*

> **Senior leader**

Our Reflecting Realities survey specifically focuses on the extent and quality of ethnic representation in children's literature. In the early phases of initiating this research, we were keen to also capture data about authorship as this is of equal importance and relevance to the case that this work has sought to make. However, through conversations with Arts Council England and the BookTrust we discovered that the BookTrust had committed to investigating this and, ever since, we have worked closely alongside our partners at BookTrust to ensure that both pieces of research are read in conjunction with one another because they in essence form two sides of the same coin. This important work led by Dr Melanie Ramdarshan Bold (2019) highlighted not only the disproportionate under-representation of authors of colour in children's publishing in the UK but also interrogated the barriers that exacerbated this. As the graphic in Figure 2.4 from the first report highlights, these barriers help to sustain an ongoing cycle of under-representation. It is therefore important that children have the opportunity to engage with creatives of colour to challenge any misconceptions and counteract this cycle.

It is important to ensure that children have the opportunity to encounter positive role models in their communities. Local trips can be a good way to open up these opportunities for children – visiting local elderly resident homes, meeting local authors or organising writing residency programmes.

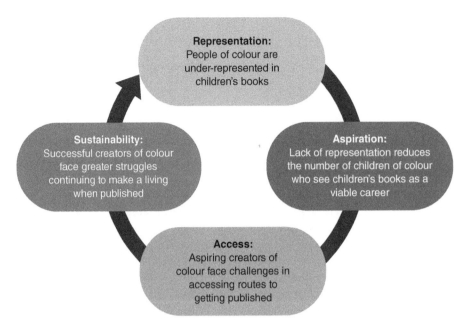

Figure 2.4 Barriers to Inclusivity among Children's Book Creators (BookTrust, Representation of people of colour among children's book authors and illustrators' Report, by Dr Melanie Ramdarshan Bold, UCL, April 2019.)

TAKE TIME TO CONSIDER

How do I ensure that the children in my school have the opportunity to encounter positive school, community and creative role models?

REFLECTING ON THE CURRENT PROVISION IN YOUR SETTING

What did this series of reflections suggest about the current provision in your setting? Where are the strengths and what areas for development might be required? If this process has helped you to identify potential actions, these will no doubt have wider implications beyond your classroom. These considerations should not be confined to one classroom alone. Inclusive practices should form the backbone of your whole school ethos, provision and culture. It is every child's entitlement to benefit from these principles at every stage of their schooling. If the framework in Figure 2.3 becomes an automated part of our considerations in the same way as considering the learning objective of a lesson, this will allow for fertile ground to empower every child in our class to truly and fully be themselves and to find and channel their voice. A class of children who feel valued and empowered will shift the dynamic in deep and profound ways resulting not only in more liberated writers, but also in a significantly elevated and enriched learning culture and community.

As will be evident from your reflections, to be inclusive we need to include all learners in all aspects of the learning experience. This means that the first and obvious place to start when considering an area of learning is with the children. So, if we are thinking about our teaching of reading then it would be appropriate to first evaluate how we and our children identify with and perceive the act of reading.

REFLECTING ON YOUR OWN READING ROUTINES

Take a moment to try to recall the last book you read. What was is about? What was its appeal? Did you enjoy it? If so, why? If not, why not? What about the story or content spoke to you? What aspects did you find less engaging? Reflecting on your text choices and reading routines, would you consider yourself to be a reader? As part of these considerations, how might you complete the following sentence, *I read because ...?* Are you an avid reader, thirsty for knowledge, who reads to deepen and expand your understanding? Books could be a source of light relief in the form of drama, comedy, adventure or escapism. They might offer comfort, personal insights, or the opportunity to better understand yourself, the world around you and your place in it. What does your completion of the sentence tell us about you as a reader? How does your relationship with reading shape and influence how you teach reading and cultivate a reading community in your class and wider school community?

If you were to invite your children to complete the same sentence, 'I read because ...' how might they answer? Would their responses differ to yours and if so in what way? You might have children who devour books and can share who and what they like to read without hesitation. Alternatively, you may have children who will in various ways convey that they read because they are directed to or expected to. The motivation in the latter instance stems from pleasing or appeasing the adult in the room, with little appreciation for the full expanse of what reading has to offer.

CULTIVATING A RELATIONSHIP WITH READING

As teachers we know that cultivating a positive relationship with reading is crucial to a child's journey towards literacy. This involves a complex process of:

- instilling and sustaining motivation
- building positive associations
- learning and applying the skills to make sense of marks on the page
- developing knowledge of how written language works
- the skills to apply their understanding to make sense of the marks on the page
- encouraging response
- conveying the purpose, value and pleasure that reading can afford them.

This is not a linear process; teachers often find themselves working with children to grapple with the challenges of all of these components simultaneously.

At the CLPE, our appreciation for the complexity of the reading process, along with the belief of the transformative benefits of being literate and having the opportunity to experience the joy that reading can bring, drives our work. We know that the process of reading is more than just the act of lifting marks from a page. Reading is a very sophisticated process which results in a multitude of cognitive, academic, social and personal benefits. Our CLPE Reading Scales provide a useful detailed breakdown of the different stages of the reading journey and the typical reading behaviours and needs at each stage of reading development. It also features guidance designed to enable teachers to incorporate practices and routines to support children along their journey towards reading competency and confidence (clpe.org.uk/research/reading-and-writing-scales).

Since the early 2000s the value of cultivating a reading for pleasure culture has been a constant feature of discourse in the primary education sector. Extensive studies have indicated the multitude of benefits that reading for pleasure can afford both in terms of the academic gains and those that go well beyond the classroom. A study conducted by Brown and Sullivan in 2013 (Sullivan and Brown, 2015) highlighted the capacity for reading for pleasure to raise standards and combat social exclusion. They found that reading for enjoyment was a more significant contributor to a child's educational success than their family's socio-economic status and that it was of more importance for a child's cognitive development between the ages of ten and 16 than their parents' level of education.

We know that being literate not only sets the foundation for better academic outcomes and improved socio-economic trajectories, but that reading can also support personal, social and emotional development, enabling better mental health and greater capacity for empathy and critical thinking. The *Literature Review* conducted by the Reading Agency (2015) distilled the multi-layered benefits and longitudinal outcomes that reading can enable.

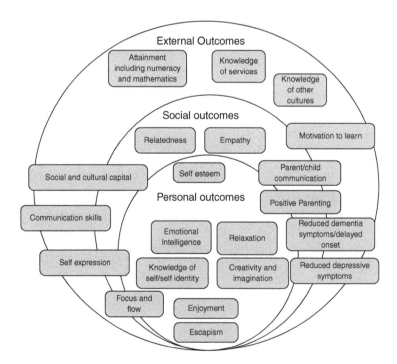

Figure 2.5 Overall Outcomes Map (The Reading Agency, Literature Review: The impact of reading for pleasure and empowerment, June 2015.)

In 2018 a study by the National Literacy Trust (Gilbert et al., 2018) indicated a positive correlation between reading proficiency and life expectancy. It suggested that being literate contributed to improved life chances and life expectancy. In 2023 Cambridge University (Sun et al., 2023) published findings that indicated that reading for pleasure contributed to better cognitive performance, mental well-being and brain structure in young adolescence. Given the life defining and changing potential that reading can provide, it therefore becomes our moral responsibility to support children to foster a positive relationship with reading and enable them to develop a positive reader identity.

The road towards becoming a literate, confident reader who has positive associations with reading can be long and challenging. The early stages of the process can involve many bumps that jolt efforts and make it hard for children to see the bigger picture of what can be gained and achieved. Our work as teachers involves striking a careful balance between developing the child's knowledge and skills base and motivating them to persist and remain enthused not just by the short-term gains but the exciting prospect of the worlds of fiction and wells of knowledge that this integral skill will open for them. Professor Teresa Cremin's (Cremin, 2020) work in this area has been key in developing our thinking around the important distinctions between the necessary skills required to support reading instruction and cultivating behaviours that support reading for pleasure.

Lighting the spark and keeping children switched onto reading involves several elements and, of course, the reading material (what children read) is integral. The right book in the right hands at the right moment can transform a child's reading journey (Drury, 1930). This is why books are a central feature of CLPE's professional development programme and are at the literal heart of our building. Our reference library houses a carefully curated set of 25,000 in-print books. We draw on this invaluable source of high-quality literature to inform and shape the design of our learning programme and teaching resources. Teachers are very adept at identifying the learning opportunities that a book might offer their children and determining the ways and extent to which it aligns with various programmes of study. Every title is unique and will add value in some shape or form to the average classroom book corner. However, we know that there are some books that are more impactful and which raise and ultimately transform the reading experience in the classroom. We've spent a great deal of time researching the features that these 'quality texts' (Meek, 1987) have in common (Ellis et al., 1996). We call them our 'core books' (clpe.org.uk/books/corebooks/corebooks-collections) and they all contain some or all of the following features:

- protagonists that children can relate to and identify with
- plots that allow opportunities to explore dilemmas, challenges, morality or ethics
- emotive storylines
- humour
- rich language
- powerful illustrations
- the capacity to blur the lines between reality and the world of the book; a book you can lose yourself in.

Writing for a young audience requires a great deal of skill. Trying to channel the right voice and strike an authentic tone in a way that will engage and sustain a young reader is a very sophisticated undertaking. Despite this, the world of children's literature has always been a rich source of titles that succeed in this endeavour and feature the key ingredients listed.

During our time at the CLPE and in our former lives as school-based practitioners, the teaching team rarely struggled to source books that featured the majority of these components. However, this was not always the case when it came to the first element, relatable protagonists.

In general, we tend to be inclined to connect. This relatability can come in the form of shared preferences or interests – a young reader might, for example, find an affinity with a character who also loathes tomatoes. A character might be of a similar age and therefore be grappling with similar experiences such as navigating the first day at school or moving to a new home. Readers might identify with the portrayal of family dynamics such as dealing with sibling rivalry or parental separation. Although a reader is likely to actively seek out and establish ways to identify with a character, the traditionally typical absence or minimal presence of characters of colour limits the opportunity for readers to relate on this important level.

One thing that we always found challenging was sourcing titles that centred and featured characters of colour. We would often have to import titles or seek out specialist booksellers to ensure that the book stock in our classrooms were broad and varied in their representations of characters of colour. This is problematic for two reasons. First, we shouldn't really have to 'seek' out books that represent a third of the child population and, second, if we are importing books from other countries then the stock of representative books will be skewed towards a narrow set of key figures and predominantly portray demographic groups and communities from other parts of the world. These representations are, of course, valuable; however, this means that there is likely to be a lack of portrayals of British marginalised demographic groups. No one community of people is a monolith. While there may be some commonalities shared across diasporas around the world, the specific geographical, historical, socio-cultural and political context of each country will inevitably influence the identities, experiences, cultures and communities within each context. Therefore, as well as importing titles that feature portrayals of racially minoritised communities outside the UK, it is important to ensure that our shelves also include specific representations of British racially minoritised communities.

THE IMPORTANCE OF REPRESENTATION

Dr Rudine Sims Bishop authored a paper in 1990 where she made the analogy of books serving as windows, mirrors and sliding glass doors; through her important body of work she has shared the transformational benefit this can have for readers. Her research is at the heart of what inspired our Reflecting Realities work. The affirming power of seeing ourselves and being seen across all art forms and areas of life is integral to our collective healthy development as individuals and as a wider society. We chose the term 'Reflecting Realities' to convey the value of reflecting the real lives of young readers within children's literature.

Throughout the formative phase of development our experiences help us to build a body of stories that shape our views of ourselves and the world around us. These stories might, in some instances be limiting, misinformed, or damaging and we may carry these impressions well into adulthood. So, in everything we do as teachers we must contemplate how we cultivate a safe and brave learning community: one that is welcoming, respectful, inclusive, challenging and aspirational. Stories and story-telling should form the backbone of primary provision and, within this, literature has an integral role to play in shaping learning. It is therefore a key resource that requires careful contemplation.

For many children, there is a disconnect between their lived realities and the realities portrayed within the books available to them, because they encounter a lack of books that reflect their sense of self, heritage, or community. This absence is compounded by significant moments that have dominated the national discourse in recent times. High-profile, often xenophobic national and international discussions focused on identity, race and Britishness will have filtered through to the children we work with, shaping their thoughts and feelings about themselves and the world around them.

What we find in the pages of books is crucial in supporting self-determination and developing critical thinking. The scope for erasure is vast and the consequences of this are severely detrimental to the health of our society and humanity. This is particularly pertinent within the context of heightened hostility towards marginalised groups which is exacerbated through policy as explored in the works of Professor Vini Lander (Lander, 2018) in her exploration of the teaching of British values and Dr Muna Abdi in her work on Somali students' school experiences (Abdi, 2022). Books therefore not only support children along their journey towards becoming literate, with all the cognitive, emotional, academic and socio-economic benefits this brings, but they also have the capacity to serve as powerful vehicles to counteract social injustice.

> Some of my children said that they'd never seen themselves reflected in a book and some of them said that they wish they had seen this. A lot of my children had said that they wish they could see more representation of Muslim people in books, women wearing hijabs. And I think just hearing our children saying that definitely made me think, okay, this is something that needed to be updated across the school.
>
> **Class teacher**

If books do not reflect the realities of the readership and the wider world then they can uphold and worsen the erasure, marginalisation, problematic or racist representations portrayed across different spheres of society. Alternatively, if our classrooms are well stocked with inclusive titles that meaningfully reflect the realities of young readers then this can support the process of counteracting racist-fuelled toxic narratives. The pull and tension of the potential for books to serve as either a force for good in this way or otherwise is summarised in the graphic in Figure 2.6.

HOW BOOKS CAN EITHER EXACERBATE OR REDRESS TOXIC NARRATIVES

Exacerbate

- Shape and uphold problematic dominant narratives
- Reinforce racism

Redress

- Challenge the normalisation of dominant, toxic narratives
- Counteract racism

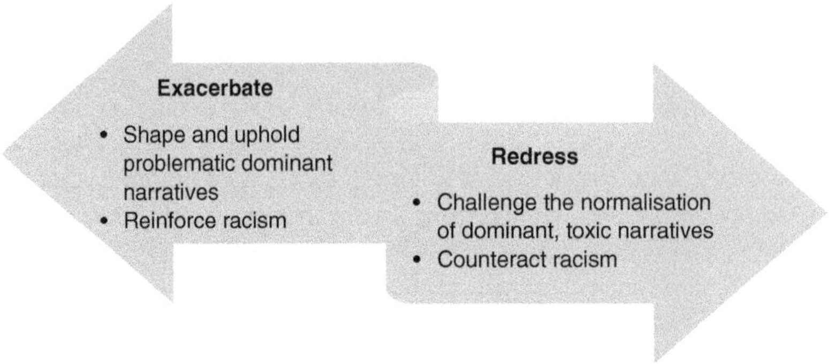

Figure 2.6   Capacity for Books to Exacerbate or Redress Toxic Narratives ©CLPE 2022/2023

The content of the books we share can pull in one of two directions and either have the capacity to uphold and exacerbate racist ideology and views or redress, expose and challenge racism and its damaging effects. Erasure from the literary canon or problematic portrayals have the potential to compromise reading experiences and children's relationship with reading, which is why what we find in the pages of the books that we encounter matters. This is also why evaluating the content of the books we share with children should go hand in hand with our work in ensuring inclusive practices and provision.

In the chapters that follow, we hope to encourage you to think deeply about what it means to be an inclusive teacher of literacy with particular regard to racial constructs and ethnicity and to consider the value of using ethnically representative books to support you in this endeavour. We will explore the intersection between policy, education and children's literature and how this can inform and shape self-perception, outlook and learner identities. We will consider the complex challenges this can pose as discussed in the *Wasafari* journal article, 'Reimagining education: where do we go from here?' (Chetty et al., 2022). To enable this, we will share what we have learnt from our Reflecting Realities work. We will share the findings from the five-year body of data we have generated at CLPE through our annual Reflecting Realities surveys (clpe.org.uk/research/reflecting-realities). By exploring what we have learnt through these reports about what constitutes quality meaningful representation of racially minoritised characters in children's literature, we will consider the implications on our classroom book stock provision. We will explore the ways in which what we find in the pages of the titles on our classroom shelves can shape children's learner, reader and writer identities. And we will consider why and how this matters. We will provide the tools to support you in reviewing your stock with this learning in mind to assist you in refining your class and wider school collections.

We will also share insights into what we have learnt from our Reflecting Realities in the Classroom-based action research project. We will outline how the combination of inclusive practices, creative teaching approaches, access to representative book stock and meaningful engagement with creatives of colour can positively impact the reading and writing development of young learners and powerfully evolve your learning culture. It will become evident that these key components are crucial ingredients in cultivating an empowering learning culture that supports children to thrive.

By sharing our learning in these key areas of our charity's work, it is our hope that this book will support you in developing inclusive teaching and learning practices in your setting. This book has been written to convey the value, necessity, means and impact of developing these practices; to ensure that every child in every classroom, wherever they may be, feels seen, heard and valued and has the best possible start on their learning journey, because when all is said and done that is all that really matters.

CHAPTER 3

DEFINING AND DEVELOPING READER IDENTITY: SHAPING LEARNERS' OUTLOOKS AND WORLD VIEW

I know from many years promoting equality in early years services that children absorb the values of the world around them. Kindness, empathy and generosity, yes, but also society's prejudices too. This damages all children. Those subject to the prejudices can internalise those stereotypes. (More than one early years worker told me tales of pre-school children of colour fighting over a 'white' doll while the 'black' doll lay discarded in the corner.) But also children from the majority culture are being shut out of new worlds of knowledge, new experiences and new friendships.

I started writing to reshape my world, I think. I grew up in multi-ethnic, non-typical families. I never saw families like mine in any books or TV programmes. Perhaps by continually writing stories with white main characters and, as I saw it, ideal married nuclear families, I could somehow write myself normal. This continued until my 30s.

Three things changed me. One was having a child and refusing to accept that she would not see herself in books. Secondly, was discovering Malorie Blackman – I can never forget the shock of seeing a British Black family in the TV adaptation of Pig Heart Boy. It gave me permission to include my own experiences in books. Third, was several years working in the not-for-profit sector and realising how the experiences of marginalised people are misrepresented and dehumanised in mainstream society.

Patrice Lawrence

Patrice Lawrence is an award-winning British writer who has published books for children of all ages. Her debut young adult (YA) novel, *Orangeboy* (Hachette, 2016), won the Bookseller YA Prize and the Waterstones Prize for Older Children's Fiction and was shortlisted for the Costa Children's Book Award. Her subsequent novels have been much acclaimed and frequent visitors to prize lists including the Jhalak Children's and Young Adult Prize 2021 and the YA Book Prize 2021. *Needle* (Barrington Stoke, 2022b) was shortlisted for the Yoto Carnegie Medal for Writing 2023 and was the winning title of the Little Rebel Awards 2023. Patrice worked for more than 20 years for charities supporting equality and social justice and she is an ambassador for the charity First Story.

The quote here is from Patrice's blog 'Granny Came Here on the Empire Windrush', written for CLPE in 2022

Find out more:

Our aspirations for the children we serve are likely to exceed those set out in national, summative assessment criteria. We want children to thrive well beyond these parameters and through creating an environment that supports children to become readers for life they will not only meet these milestones but surpass them.

> *I think for me the most important thing was just giving children the agency and letting them feel that they were allowed to be proud of who they were and create something that represented them.*

Class teacher

In the previous chapter, we spent time contemplating what it meant to feel truly included and to be part of a learning community that gives permission and opportunity for children to bring their whole being into the classroom space. This supports children to feel that they belong, that their perspective matters and that their contributions are valued. This in turn encourages them to have the inclination and confidence to participate, try things out, take risks and form the important building blocks for a healthy learner identity.

Additionally, we also considered the components that should form the foundation of inclusive practice and reflected on how we nurture learner identity and foster an inclusive learning culture. In this chapter, we will explore the concept of reader identity, the implications of this on our practice and how we need to consider reader identity when we are thinking about reflecting realities in the literacy classroom and literary space.

To recognise yourself as a reader you need the competency and confidence to apply your knowledge and skills to the process and a willingness to practise, refine and develop those skills. We can break this down further into five key facets that ultimately combine to inform and shape a person's reader identity, as detailed in the graphic in Figure 3.1. We are going to look at each of these components in turn.

THE KEY COMPONENTS OF READER iDENTiTY

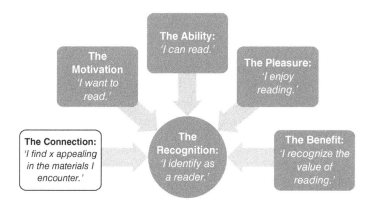

Figure 3.1   Key Components of Reader Identity ©CLPE 2022/2023

THE MOTIVATION

If we want children to engage with and consume the contents of our classroom book corners, then the stock needs to be appetising. Reading tastes and preferences are as unique as every individual and will vary and evolve over time. In their formative phase of development, the evolving interests of young readers will sit alongside their developing reading competency. As their knowledge and understanding of the reading process grows and they hone their skills, they require reading materials that not only support their development and confidence but also keep them motivated to persist. So, when we talk about breadth and range of stock there are many defining layers. In the first instance we must have a range of text types and reading materials containing a breadth of themes with varied and appealing age-appropriate subject matter. These should include but not be limited to story props, board games, card games, comics, magazines, newspapers, annuals, joke books, picturebooks, graphic novels, short story collections, chapter books, novels, poetry collections and verse novels. As well as covering a range of themes and areas of interest our collections should encompass a variety of genres and writing styles. By offering a broad range of choice of text types we are helping young readers to learn to browse, to try new reading matter and to develop their understanding of themselves as readers.

> *Having this stock of representative literature available in our school means that even our youngest children are actually stopping and thinking about what they want to read and making those choices.*

Class teacher

Offering this range of choice becomes even more important when we are working in a context where cuts to library services and the implications of national and global recession are compromising children's access to a range of quality texts. For some children, the classroom will be the sole source of book access and against this challenging backdrop teachers play an even more crucial role as the gatekeepers of literature.

> *I think that my children were able to find reading material that they enjoyed in the past, but I'm not sure whether they felt a personal connection to it as I don't think that there were enough representative texts to enable this previously. Since being on the project, we've spent a lot of time filling our library with much more diverse texts, much more inclusive texts and I can't see any of them in the library now because they've all been taken out! So I think that's definitely a good sign as it is clear that these books interest the children. These are books that they really enjoy.*

Class teacher

THE ABILITY

Reading is not a skill that children will naturally acquire; it is a skill that must be explicitly taught. It is a cognitively demanding and complex process that requires a great deal of risk taking, stamina and resilience. In the early stages of acquiring this skill, we don't always necessarily appreciate how all the different components work or how they fit together. We might struggle to hold all the different parts together and navigate them to help us make sense of the text before us. The demands of the process can make it challenging to appreciate the bigger picture, almost like staring intensely at the bark of a tree to comprehend what we're seeing without appreciating the vastness of the forest that we're standing in. Our book stock needs to contain titles that entice and encourage children to stick with the process but are also varied in their degrees of challenge.

The gradation of challenge is crucial in supporting children to feel empowered to keep investing the effort while also appropriately stretching them over time. This means our book corners need to contain a range of text types of varying substance, length and sophistication that support the acquisition of the technical skills that enable us to become a reader. We need texts that have strong narrative structures, patterned, rhythmic language, repetitive text and sophisticated interplay between words and pictures. Texts like these support children in building a set of associations and expectations that enable them to better anticipate what might be coming up. They can test their theories based on content they have encountered before and build a foundation of confidence to tackle the unknown.

In these early stages of becoming a reader, children can be self-conscious about how far they might be from acquiring the goal of literacy, particularly if they perceive their peers to be ahead of them in the game. This means that ensuring that a book contains these supportive elements should not come at the cost of the quality of the content. If the substance of the title feels patronising or diluted at the expense of fulfilling these requirements, then children will notice this. There is an element of vulnerability involved in learning to read and it is important to not exacerbate this by making a child unnecessarily self-conscious by restricting their access to books that might be perceived as being aimed at younger readers.

THE PLEASURE

We know through the extensive research (Krashen, 2004) in this area that cultivating a reading for pleasure culture is crucial to habituating the act of reading. If young readers experience the comfort, joy, suspense, thrills, drama, escape and world-expanding capacity of books then we no longer need to make a case for why it is a skill worth investing in. Through our routines of book sharing, we model and provide children with the opportunity to experience the pleasure that can be derived from books. The texts that we curate to support this must offer access to a range of literary genres as this will broaden the scope for children to be intellectually challenged and have a range of emotional responses and experiences through the literature they encounter. They need to build positive associations that help them to appreciate the entertainment value that books can afford.

We've done a lot of work on the Valerie Bloom unit of study. Her voice, her accent, her word choices, her turns of phrases sound like lots of our children's parents. She sounds like their aunties and sounds like their grans. She sounds and feels familiar. The food that she talks about in her poetry gets them excited and they'll say things like, 'Oh, I love rice and peas.' They understand and know the language and meanings because they share the same background and appreciate the Caribbean influences in her writ-ing. I feel like books and authors that are not just representative of wider society, but are specifically representative of our school community, encourage a deeper and more powerful connection.

Class teacher

THE BENEFIT

As educators and literate adults, we are aware of the multi-layered personal, social, emo-tional, cognitive and academic benefits of reading. In Chapter 2 we discussed the research that highlights these benefits. When a child is in the early stages of acquiring the skill of reading they are not going to appreciate these long-term, wide-ranging advantages because the short-term challenges overshadow the layered and long-term gains. The texts available to children must therefore not only create opportunity for pleasurable engagement but must also empower children to seek out information to feed their curiosity, challenge their think-ing, broaden their knowledge and deepen their learning. Having the time to engage with such texts both independently and through mediated sessions will enable children to expe-rience the benefits first-hand. High-quality non-fiction reading materials that present information in creative, varied and innovative ways in different formats and aesthetic styles are therefore an important component of your book corner.

We have one copy of Black and British *by David Olusoga (2020) in the class. One child, a Black child sourced a second-hand copy of the title for herself because the class copy of the book was on loan to another child. She offered to loan her copy to her friend and encouraged her to take it home for the weekend as we had a weekend coming up. I thought that was extremely powerful. I hadn't realised that because someone was read-ing our sole class copy that she had taken it upon herself to buy a second-hand copy. This shows the power of just letting children know what's available and allowing them access through our book corners. The fact that she shared her copy with another child showed how passionate she was about a book. The other child who was also very recep-tive grabbed the chance and wanted to read it. There was a sense that the book offered an affirmation of their heritage, and they were keen to learn more. There was a real sense of pride which I think is so important.*

Class teacher

THE CONNECTION

The act of reading at its core is about using our knowledge of how written language works to interpret the meaning of the text by drawing on the breadth of knowledge and experience at our disposal. The work of Aidan Chambers (2011) has formed the corner-stone of CLPE's work on developing reader response with the schools we've worked with.

It has been evident through this work that encouraging children to make connections to what they read by drawing on personal associations, lived experiences and inter-textual links is fundamental to supporting them to make sense of texts and tap into the deeper layers of meaning. Arguably, we can read without personally connecting to the substance of the reading material or at least achieve meaning by only making surface-level connections that help us to interpret the text. However, personal connection is a key component to supporting a deeper and more meaningful engagement with texts. As Dr Rudine Sims Bishop (1990) commented, *Literature transforms human experience and reflects it back to us, and in that reflection, we can see our own lives and experiences as part of the larger human experience*. Failing to provide the opportunity to enable this short-changes the reader and places a ceiling on the heights of value that the reading experience has the potential to create.

When studying Ken Wilson-Max's picturebook, Where's Lenny? *(2020), I noticed one boy in particular was struck by the likeness of the main character Lenny. He looked at that character and thought, that's me, or that was me as a really young child. And instantly just became far more engaged in the lessons than he had done in previous English lessons. There have been lots of times during this project when we'd read a book, we'd share it together and then children would go home and they'd come in with another book and comment on the similarities between the characters and how they looked.*

Class teacher

They were a lot keener to talk and share their thoughts, particularly when we did the Valerie Bloom unit and looked at the hair-inspired poems. I had a couple of girls, one girl in particular, who would always wear her hair tied back. Soon after we'd studied the poem about hair and talked about the experience of the mum combing hair, discussing details such as the length of time it takes, the pain and different feelings, the types of combs and particular hair products required, she then came in with her hair completely out, which she'd never done before. So I think that throughout the project there were these small but important moments when I thought: that's had a real impact on particular children.

Class teacher

The distance a reader needs to travel to make a personal connection will vary from person to person. We may not have walked the streets of Victorian Britain but sadly we are probably able to draw on extensive contemporary examples of child poverty in the UK and around the world to support our understanding of the depictions of this phenomenon in literature set in the period. In connecting with characters, their dilemmas and their world, we draw on what we know. The well of associations for younger readers will be somewhat confined compared to an adult reader simply by virtue of the fact that they haven't lived long enough to build as extensive a body of knowledge, experiences and references. Therefore, in the process of making sense of texts they must start with who they are and what they know.

When we shared Where's Lenny? *there were certain children that really identified with the book because it was the first time a lot of them had seen a book with a character of colour in and they could really identify with it. The illustrations were very obviously representative of a culture and family dynamic that children could relate to. We used* Look Up *(Bryon and Adeola, 2019) with Year 2 and some of the children obviously, once again, were able to identify with the illustration, especially the hair scene. There was a real sense of, 'we can talk about that'. We have seen a lot of firsts. There have been a number of times in which children have seen a representation they could relate to for the first time. In one instance I recall sharing a book with a Year 6 child and it was the first time she'd seen a character that looked like her.*

Senior leader

Writers of children's literature work hard to create relatable, interesting and inspiring story worlds. How young readers relate will vary. A character's traits or personality might resonate, the setting might feel familiar, or they might connect because of friendship dynamics or family make-up. We also know that readers also make connections with characters that look like them, have backgrounds that are recognisable, live in places that strike a familiar chord or experiences that are relatable to their own. The absence or marginalisation of characters of colour that has traditionally been a feature of children's literature means that the opportunity to make connections based on facets of identity like language, ethnicity and culture have traditionally been less available to readers from racially minoritised backgrounds, thus potentially compromising the experience of connection for many young readers.

There are certain children across the school who are seeking out representative books. There's one child in particular who's in Year 3 who really struggled with the phonic screening check and I would say previously didn't enjoy reading. I've noticed that when she has the opportunity to choose her reading for pleasure book each week she consistently picks books that feature characters that look like her. She's one child that stands out in my mind but I feel like this is the case for lots of children across the school, who are seeking out representative books with characters that look like them.

Senior leader

In her book *The Dark Fantastic* (2019), Professor Ebony Thomas discusses the ceiling that such absence places on imaginary worlds and describes this failing as an 'imagination gap' – a gap that leaves readers short-changed and can contribute to the idea that these fictional worlds are exclusive domains that are the entitlement of some and not all. In later chapters, we will go on to explore the implications of this in terms of how children might internalise this erasure and how this might shape their impressions of the literary space and their engagement with it.

Across the schools participating in the Reflecting Realities in the Classroom research project, we have had the privilege of witnessing first-hand the surprise, the glee and the warmth of feeling that encountering characters of colour has inspired in many young readers. This affirmation not only enriches the reading experience by allowing for the opportunity to connect more deeply and meaningfully, but it also legitimises the presence of characters of colour in the literary space, thereby counteracting their traditional omission or marginalisation and the problematic conclusions that might be drawn from this. Engaging with the works of creatives of colour who have imbued their work with rich linguistic and cultural references has added a rich depth and meaningfulness to the reading experience of the participating classes.

Valerie Bloom had a huge impact, particularly regarding the way she draws on her language and heritage. We have quite a few children that have Caribbean heritage, so for them to see a poet from Jamaica and hear her delivering poetry in Patois was huge, because they all recognise that language straight away and actually felt empowered to think, I can write like this and I can represent myself in this way.

Class teacher

COMBINING THE FIVE FACETS

When these five components work in harmony with one another, with children having the opportunity to:

* meaningfully connect to reading materials
* feel motivated and capable to access texts
* derive positive experiences that allow them to see and value the benefit

then they not only appreciate what reading can do for them but they are also more likely to be able to recognise themselves as readers.

It is evident and obvious that those who read often, read well. This is why cultivating strong reading routines and a positive reading culture is fundamental to supporting children to habituate the act of reading. Through our teaching of reading, we dedicate enormous efforts into equipping children with the knowledge and skills while sustaining their motivation to persist. The personal, emotional and social gains detailed in the previous chapter highlight the enriching potential that the act of reading can create. The intensity of pace and density of content coverage required of primary teachers might, at times, mean that these outcomes are likely to be fortuitous by-products as opposed to core aims. In the teaching of reading, it is important to consider how what we do and don't do shapes the child's sense of themselves as a reader. We can be quick to ask if a child can read, or how well they can read, but how often do we ask about the extent to which the child identifies as a reader?

Take a moment to reconsider the five facets of reader identity (Figure 3.1). Which elements of the graphic do you invest most of your teaching time in supporting children to develop? Conversely, which elements do you spend less time working on with your children? What are some of the ways in which you support the development of these areas?

When we work with teachers at the CLPE we usually find that the connection component is the less developed area. Although teachers will make efforts to source and use texts that children can relate to in various ways, we have found that this is not often the dominant driver for text selection. And if it is, the relatability component hasn't traditionally always been focused on the inclusion of characters of colour. A lack of consideration in this area is a missed opportunity on a number of levels.

Our research has shown us what we have known from anecdotes from teachers for many years – one book can ignite a passion for reading and transform a child's relationship with reading. And we also know that connection is key to this. In the schools on the Reflecting Realities in the Classroom programme we have been able to document children's deepening and developing reader identity because they are able to see themselves in texts. Participating teachers have highlighted the value of the affirmation children felt as a result of feeling represented in the texts in their schools and the ways in which they had connected with characters or settings which they hadn't been doing before the programme.

> *This work has positively impacted their aspirations in terms of reading. I think, the changes we've made and the texts that we have made available in school for them to read have made a real difference. For some of the children that might have been reluctant or perhaps fluent readers, but just didn't find something that they connected with, they are just devouring books now.*

Class teacher

> *The Dapo Adeola books have been very popular and the character Rocket, in particular, has really resonated with lots of our children.* Look Up! *(Bryon and Adeola, 2019) has been a massive, massive hit as a core unit title and as part of our reading for pleasure collection from which it's probably the most picked book. Rocket looks like our children, she has the same hair, the same skin tone and is the same age as a lot of our children. From the front cover and in every detail, it makes a really important visual statement.*

Class teacher

The benefit of inclusive and representative texts serves readers from marginalised communities by providing a source of affirmation. It also benefits readers from all and every background because to understand and be understood is at the heart of the human experience. The space between what is written and what is read is a safe space in which we can make sense of our lives and the world around us. Art and life interchangeably mirror and echo one another. Books offer readers opportunities to influence, shape and make sense of their world; when world and political events mean that we are living through uncertain and polarising times, finding content within the pages of books that counteracts this and helps us to process what is happening is even more important.

TOOLS TO SUPPORT YOU TO CONSIDER YOUR PROVISION IN TERMS OF READER IDENTITY

Having considered the facets that comprise reader identity, we'd like to invite you to consider how the provision in your setting supports children to develop these different facets. Take a moment to consolidate your thinking. Create a table to use as a review tool, using the example shown in Figure 3.2 to help you.

CLPE tool to review how our provision supports the different components of reader identity

| | Book stock | How is each component fostered through... | | |
		Reading routines, e.g. independent reading time, reading aloud sessions, group reading	Taught reading programme	Wider learning provision	School community reading routines, e.g. book clubs, assembly story time, reading buddies
Connection					
Motivation					
Ability					
Pleasure					
Benefit					

Figure 3.2 ©CLPE 2023

What is the weighting in each area? What do you dedicate most of your time investing in? What do your reflections suggest about which aspects of the reading process are valued? And how might these shape perceptions of what reading is and how children identify with it?

FACTORS TO CONSIDER IN DEVELOPING READER IDENTITY

We invest a great deal of time in supporting children to develop the knowledge and skills to be able to read. We work hard to keep them motivated through our choices of teaching approaches and the design of our lessons. Through story-sharing routines, directed reading opportunities and thoughtfully stocked and carefully organised book corners we try to convey the pleasure that reading can afford. Through these efforts and a high-quality, comprehensive literacy programme of study children will learn to recognise the value and understand the benefit and in doing so will, over time, come to see themselves as a readers. They will see themselves as a readers because they are simultaneously motivated, capable and confident while also experiencing the pleasure and recognising the value.

Reflect on the extent to which these different facets manifest in the children in your class. Is there a disproportionate prominence in certain facets over others? Are there common patterns across your class of children? To help you ponder these questions, select three children at random, think about what you know about how they engage with reading during independent free-reading sessions and what your observations tell you about their capabilities. Use the table in Figure 3.3 to give an estimated score in each category from zero to five, zero indicating the lowest score and five indicating the highest. You may find that you need to spend some time observing the children before deciding an appropriate score for a particular facet. Jot down any comments that you feel might be useful in supporting your considerations.

Based on your existing knowledge, what do the scores suggest about each reader? Does the balance across the different facets vary? If so, how and what might this indicate? How do the scores compare across the group? Are there similarities or differences? Do any patterns arise? What might these indicate about the readers or the reading provision? What might you want to explore to support improvements to these scores?

REVIEWING PROVISION AND PRACTICE TO DEVELOP READER IDENTITY

Now take a moment to pause and consider how, through your practice, you support children to develop these different facets; use the framework in Figure 3.4 to note your thoughts and evaluate your reading provision.

What insights have these three exercises revealed about the children, practice and provision in your setting? What facets of reader identity are more strongly embedded, and which require more development? Does any aspect of the practice and provision hinder or enable these different facets and, if so, in what ways?

It may not be the case in all instances, but it is likely that the elements of reader identity that scored higher were in the areas of motivation, ability, pleasure and benefit. This will be because it is easier to observe and determine these and also because these are typically the dimensions of reader identity that are most likely to be nurtured within the traditional school curriculum. We tend to spend a larger proportion of our time creating a learning environment that is conducive to supporting the development of these strands of reader identity. In our work, we tend to see less time dedicated to enabling connection than we do to the other areas of reader identity.

CLPE reader identity review tool

	Child A	Child B	Child C
How strongly does the child identify with the reading materials available?	Score:	Score:	Score:
	Comment:	Comment:	Comment:
How sustained is the child's motivation?	Score:	Score:	Score:
	Comment:	Comment:	Comment:
How competent is the child in their reading ability in line with age-related expectations?	Score:	Score:	Score:
	Comment:	Comment:	Comment:
How much do they enjoy reading?	Score:	Score:	Score:
	Comment:	Comment:	Comment:
To what extent do they recognise the value of reading?	Score:	Score:	Score:
	Comment:	Comment:	Comment:
Note the total score out of a potential of 25 and any overall comments			

Figure 3.3   ©CLPE 2023

Each interaction with a book has the potential to spark a connection; how and, as we have expressed, what we connect to will differ from person to person and from book to book. Try to recall the last time you were in a library or a book shop. What kind of browser are you? Do you know exactly what you're looking for and race straight towards the relevant section? Do you like random discoveries and so spend your time dipping in and out of titles that catch your eye? What kinds of books are you drawn to? Do you read to learn more about the world, or do you read to escape it? Do you like a fast-paced novel or a story that takes its time to unfold? Do you read to learn more about yourself or to help you understand others? Your responses to these questions will vary on any given day and certainly over time; however, they give an indication as to why you read and the kind of reader you are. The connections you form with a book might be based on the subject matter, setting, period, dilemmas, or characters. The style of writing, use of regional dialect, familiar turns of phrase or names of people or places might be another source of connection.

CLPE reading provision review tool

	How does your class book stock provision support children to:	How do your book-sharing routines at home and in the classroom support children to:	How does your core literacy programme of study support children to:	How do your whole-school routines support children to:
cultivate connection with books/ reading?				
feel motivated to read?				
develop their competency as readers?				
derive pleasure from reading?				
appreciate the benefits of reading?				

Figure 3.4 ©CLPE 2023

If you were to ask your children what they enjoy reading and what it is about the books they read that appeals, it is likely that you would receive a range of responses – from children who struggle to identify particular texts and simply name the last book the class studied to appease you to children who will have a very clear idea about what they like and why. Just as for adults, children will connect with books in a range of ways. They may connect because of the deliciousness of the humour; they might relate to the age of the protagonist, or the experiences being relayed, or the dilemmas being explored. The power of connection cannot be underestimated because we know through our work with schools that the right book at the right time can have tremendously transformative benefits for a child's reading journey. We have seen first-hand many instances in which a specific book ignited a spark in a child in a way that totally changed their view of themselves as readers, shifted the way they engaged with reading and altered their outlook.

Given the unique and varied ways in which we have the potential to connect to texts, it is all the more important to ensure our class book corner is brimming with a broad and varied book stock – titles that encompass a range of genres, text types, set in a range of real and fictional places, across time periods, touching on a variation of subject matter and themes and written in a range of formats and styles. We will spend time browsing the shelves of your book corner in the next chapter and considering how, budgets permitting, the stock could be developed and enriched.

CONNECTION AND IDENTITY

We've touched on the range of ways in which we might connect to texts as readers and what might draw us to a book and keep us hooked. In our work we have seen that a core component of connection is the connection that is derived from seeing yourself on the page. Dr Rudine Sims Bishop's important body of work has been instrumental in developing thinking in this area. Her analogy of books having the scope to serve as mirrors, windows and sliding doors serves as an enlightening and very useful means of understanding the transformative affirming and enriching potential of books. Through her extensive study of children's literature featuring African American casts of characters she determined that the quality of casting and content could enable the opportunity to serve as a reflection of the reader's life by mirroring facets of physical, experiential, familial, social, cultural, linguistic and other relatable identifiers. By serving as a mirror a book can go beyond being a tool for entertainment or information; on a fundamental level it affirms the reader's sense of self. This validation taps into a deeper layer of connection that enthuses the reader, enriches the reading experience and arguably strengthens the bond with reading and, by extension, this facet of reader identity. Dr Sims Bishop's work also emphasises the value of inclusive representative literature as being crucial for all readers. She does this by extending her analogy by also talking about books in terms of their function as windows and sliding doors. Windows into lived experiences beyond our own and sliding doors that enable us to slip into spaces and places beyond our own realm of reference. The opportunities that books afford us to take a look and wander into these spaces offer another important layer of enrichment and scope to deepen our knowledge, challenge our thinking and broaden our outlook.

Therefore, to nurture reader identity in the most holistic sense we must think carefully about the content of the books on our classroom shelves and the books that make up the core of our reading, literacy and wider programmes of study. Every book that sits in your book corner, every book that you choose to use as a focus text, every book you select to share with children will be perceived as an endorsement. It will indicate to the children what you value as having merit and being worthy of engagement. If these texts are void of the inclusion and representation of racially minoritised characters, then what does this convey and how might this compromise the affirming and enriching potential of books as outlined by Dr Sims Bishop's work?

How might this impact on the development of children's reader identity and how might we optimise the opportunity that ethnically inclusive texts afford us in raising a generation of secure, resilient, happy, enlightened, critically reflective and sophisticated readers? As we move through this book we will continue to return to these questions to help steer our thinking; in the next chapter we will look at the key considerations and practical actions that need to be taken when you are thinking about the very real issues of how you ensure that you are creating a literacy environment that encourages connection for all children.

The children see themselves in the books they're reading, which is the result of the careful curation of texts that we've been supported to develop. They like to share their interests and hobbies, but also the personal connections of how the characters look and feel, about family make-up and things that they feel represent them in a story. And you can see the passion they have for visiting the library and their book corners, the way they want to recommend books to each other and how they speak to adults about books. And they will come and ask, I've read this, this part of a series; can you order me the next one?

Class teacher

CHAPTER 4

REVIEWING AND DEVELOPING AN INCLUSIVE STOCK OF BOOKS

> My upbringing in Roehampton on the Alton Estate has been a huge influence. It was the eighties and me and my friends would regularly play out and make believe and have adventures, so I got to explore a lot, probably far more than kids get to do nowadays. There are settings in Roehampton that I return to in my work because they hold a certain fascination, a sense that magic could have been real there. I am also greatly influenced by family life and the realization that families like my own (single parent, working class) were so often left out of stories. I always wanted to visit Narnia, but bemoaned the fact I didn't have a big house or a huge wooden wardrobe ... Narnia felt closed to me.
>
> Joseph Coelho

Joseph Coelho is an award-winning performance poet, playwright and children's and Waterstone's Children Laureate 2022–4. His debut poetry collection *Werewolf Club Rules* (Frances Lincoln, 2014) was the winner of the CLPE Poetry Award (CLiPPA) 2015. His work has poetry and performance at its heart, drawing on over 20 years' experience running dynamic creative literacy sessions in schools. He aims to inspire young people through stories and characters they can recognise and explores themes including fear, courage, diversity, gratitude, empathy and loss. Joe writes for children of all ages; his picture books include the critically acclaimed *Luna Loves ...* series illustrated by Fiona Lumbers (Andersen Press, 2017–23) and *If All the World Were ...* illustrated by Allison Colpoys (Lincoln Children's Books, 2018), which won the Independent Bookshop Week Book Award 2019. His work across poetry includes the collection *Overheard in a Tower Block* (Otter-Barry Books, 2017), which was shortlisted for the CLiPPA 2018, and *The Girl Who Became a Tree* (Otter-Barry Books, 2019), which was shortlisted for the 2021 Carnegie Medal. Other work includes his middle-grade series *Fairytales Gone Bad*, illustrated by Freya Hartas (Walker, 2020–2) and YA novel *The Boy Lost in the Maze* (Otter-Barry Books, 2022), as well as non-fiction titles including *How to Write Poems*, illustrated by Matt Robertson (Bloomsbury, 2017). In addition to exploring emotional landscapes, Joseph is inspired by magic, the ancient world and often draws on his own experiences transforming them into something universal that can be shared. Throughout his career he has highlighted the power of poetry and reading; he is a patron of the CLPE

The quote here is from Joe's blog about *Fairy Tales Gone Bad*, written for CLPE in 2021.

Find out more:

In Chapter 3, we looked at why access to a breadth and range of quality literature should be considered an entitlement for children and a core component of every school's provision. In primary school classrooms, the book corner plays a very important role and forms the basis of the classroom reading diet. One in seven state primary schools does not have a library and we know that national library provision is diminishing (National Literacy Trust, 2022). School budgets have suffered greatly in recent years, and we know from our work that there are so many pressures on spending; many schools are finding it difficult to allocate budget to book stock. These factors place a greater weight of responsibility on classroom bookshelves to deliver, particularly given that in some instances this might be the only source of literature available to the children in our schools.

Within this context, our role as the curators of our classroom book corners is all the more important. The books we make available to our children need to showcase the breadth of what the act of reading can offer. We can channel children's curiosity through reading as it supports them to acquire information and build their knowledge by answering and inviting questions. Reading provides an important source of entertainment, offering children opportunities to escape, relax, laugh out loud, hang on the edge of their seats or go on an adventure. It can support children to form connections, develop empathy and learn more about the world around them to better understand their place in it. Reading also offers an important means of challenging thinking by exposing children to new ideas that can invite them to reflect on and re-evaluate their perspective.

The extent of how inclusive and representative the titles we stock in our classrooms are might not always form part of the first level of considerations in schools and can sometimes occur as an afterthought or coincide with seasonal reviews prompted by religious festivals or celebrations such as Black History Month. If we don't make this an integral part of considerations when building and refining our book stock, this can potentially result in a lack of stock or inadvertently marginalising inclusive titles to an exclusive 'diverse' shelf.

> *Only 1 per cent of our books represented our children. About half our school is not white British, but yet they were not represented in our books. This has been the biggest focus for us, and we've shared that with staff to open their eyes to actually realise why this is important. There were a lot of questions about, why are we doing this, whether it was tokenistic. But we know that our children are going to benefit from this and that has been the driving force behind it.*

Class teacher

Depending on our starting points, the task of curating a broad and balanced stock of representative literature might feel like an overwhelming undertaking. The graphic in Figure 4.1 offers a series of prompts to encourage considerations about the varying functions of reading. It shows what reading supports us to be able to do and can be used to guide our evaluation of the extent to which our existing stock offers these opportunities. These prompts can encourage us to also consider how effectively our books achieve these functions and inform our future text selections.

FUNCTIONS OF READING

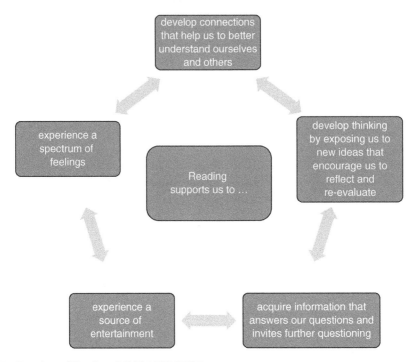

Figure 4.1   Functions of Reading ©CLPE 2022/2023

These multiple functions can form the foundation of helping us to determine *what* to stock. By asking whether we have books that invite these opportunities we can begin to ascertain how rich and varied what we have on offer actually is.

> *There were examples of representation which had been put in deliberately, but we defi-nitely felt like it wasn't enough and it wasn't necessarily consistent. So some year groups have more than others. Certainly, it was stronger in the fiction strand. We didn't really have any representative poetry or non-fiction.*

Class teacher

In this chapter, we will look at what we have learnt from five years of researching the output of the children's publishing industry in the UK and how what we know can help you to think about the book stock in your classrooms. We'll share some of the findings from the research and also some tools and questions that we have found valuable in our work.

As we discussed in the previous chapter, it is crucial to ensure that we offer a range of text types and genres, covering a variety of subject matter and themes, produced in varied, creative and innovative formats, encompassing a host of different writing and illustration styles produced by creatives from a range of backgrounds. We will naturally also want to contemplate how what we stock complements our programmes of study to support wider reading and enrich children's learning.

In 2022, we published the fifth report in our annual Reflecting Realities survey series (CLPE, 2022). Having a five-year data set enabled us to illustrate the growth of output of ethnically representative and inclusive children's literature over time. The contrast of 4 per cent of children's literature featuring racially minoritised characters in the first year to 20 per cent in the fifth indicates a remarkable rate of growth.

EXTENT OF PRESENCE OF CHARACTERS OF COLOUR IN CHILDREN'S LITERATURE PUBLISHED IN THE UK OVER FIVE- YEAR PERIOD

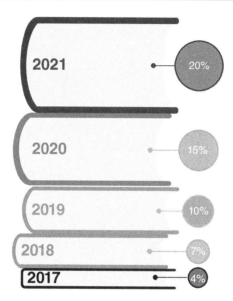

Figure 4.2   Percentage of Children's Books Published featuring Racially Minoritised Characters (Reflecting Realities Survey 2021) ©CLPE 2022/2023

With that said, it is important to remain mindful that volume alone is not a sufficient marker of progress; meaningful representation must also be determined by quality. While there has been growth in all areas that we monitor through the Reflecting Realities survey, it is worth interrogating elements of the findings to reflect on the implications they have on the choices we make in our classrooms. As part of the review process, we read picturebooks, fiction and non-fiction as these text types make up the core of the book corner stock in primary school classrooms.

PERCENTAGE OF RACIALLY MINORITISED CHARACTERS FEATURING IN UK CHILDREN'S FICTION, NON-FICTION AND PICTUREBOOKS OVER THE LAST FIVE YEARS

Although there has been incremental growth of presence within each text type, we have noted a consistent and widening gap in growth between picturebooks and fiction and non-fiction. We have also noted the relatively slow increase in presence of characters of colour in fiction compared to picturebooks and non-fiction. In the first two reporting cycles the difference between the text types was not very large. However, since the third report we have found the rate of growth in the presence of racially minoritised groups in fiction compared to the other two text types to be markedly slower, with the gap significantly widening over time. This disparity means that we need to look harder for good-quality representative fiction and that we must also look carefully at the representative picturebooks on offer. We must be discerning, and we offer some guidance to support you to achieve that later on in this chapter.

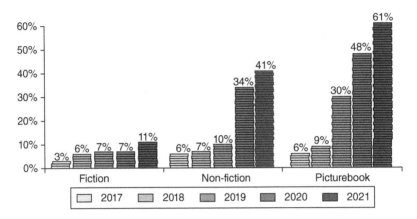

Figure 4.3 Percentage of Racially Minoritised Characters featuring in UK Children's Fiction, Non-fiction and Picturebooks ©CLPE 2022

Although we appear to have more choice, the extent of the quality within this volume of output is quite varied. In the hundreds of picturebooks we reviewed for the last survey, for example, we encountered a breadth of presence which ranged from barely present or problematic depictions to exceptionally well-rendered portrayals.

SPECTRUM OF QUALITY OF PRESENCE IN PICTUREBOOKS

We want readers to encounter characters with agency, who are identifiable, relatable, nuanced, varied and central to the narrative. Based on our observations, the quality of portrayals of characters of colour in picturebooks continues to tend to sit on a spectrum of vague, at worst, to great, at best. On one end of the spectrum, we continued to encounter titles in which there was barely any presence or the presence was too ambiguous to determine; on the opposite end of the spectrum we were delighted to read carefully crafted, distinctive titles.

As part of the Reflecting Realities review we also spend time determining the quality of the depiction of characters of colour. We consider their position in the narrative, their contribution to the plot, the extent of their agency, how they have been characterised, the cast dynamics and any other details that convey an impression about the individual.

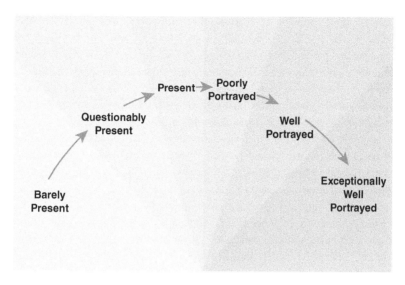

Figure 4.4   Spectrum of Presence in Picturebooks ©CLPE 2022

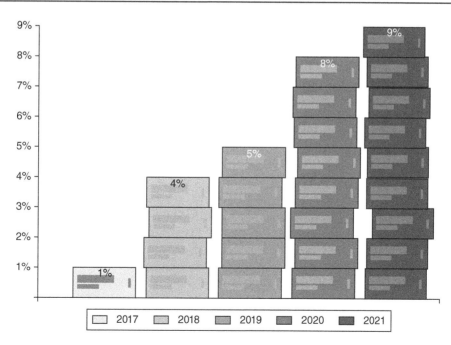

Figure 4.5   Children's books published featuring a main character from a racially minoritised background ©CLPE 2022

The increase of representative titles published between 2017 and 2021 also corresponds with an increase in the presence of racially minoritised characters forming part of the main cast. Nine per cent of the children's books published in the UK in 2021 had a main character from a racially minoritised background, compared to 8 per cent in 2020, 5 per cent in 2019, 4 per cent in 2018 and 1 per cent in 2017. As the 9 per cent figure indicates, we are continuing to see a slow but positive growth in the number of children's books featuring a main character from a racially minoritised background.

Over the five years of the Reflecting Realities study, as the volume of titles we review has increased, so too has the variation of portrayals of characters of colour. As welcome as this increase is, it should be viewed with cautious optimism – first, because it remains a very low figure and, second, because we cannot risk complacency at this point.

Through access to quality representative and inclusive literature, younger readers have the opportunity to experience the world as it is, as well as enjoy the possibilities of how it could be. The connections, enthusiasm, curiosity and awe that characters have the capacity to inspire in young readers mean that careful attention must be paid to how these characters have been crafted.

The vast volume of children's books published every year combined with how time-deprived classroom teachers are, can make the process of reviewing and curating stock feel like an overwhelming undertaking. As the range and number of titles has increased, the challenge for the contemporary classroom practitioner has become less about sourcing representative literature and instead more about distinguishing quality representations from light touch or poorly executed portrayals.

DEGREES OF ERASURE

When we are reviewing and choosing books at CLPE we spend a great deal of time looking at the quality of representation in the books we receive. The year on year increase in figures for books featuring characters of colour in the Reflecting Realities surveys implies a higher visibility of racially minoritised characters, but during our reviews we realised that the increase masked a worrying phenomenon. We were struck by the range of ways in which characters of colour were effectively rendered 'visibly invisible' and we encountered repeated instances in which the presence of characters of colour was diminished. We identified patterns across texts that highlighted some of the ways in which characters of colour were actively marginalised and developed a glossary of terms that helped define these common patterns and articulate instances in which the inclusion of characters of colour was compromised by the quality, or nature, of their presence in the text.

Each term was created to convey the type of erasure observed in the titles we reviewed. This lexicon has proven to be helpful in encouraging critical reflection and enabling us to articulate the features of texts that can undermine the quality of representation. We have also found that these terms and their accompanying definitions have been useful to others who want to describe, talk about or discuss the content of the books in book corners and libraries so we share them with you here.

COUNTRY-SPECIFIC SETTING WITHOUT COUNTRY-SPECIFIC POPULATION

This refers to instances in books where it was evident that a scene is located in a specific part of the world outside the UK, but the characters present are exclusively or predominantly white, rendering the Indigenous population invisible: for example, portrayals of countries in the African continent where readers encounter exclusively white characters or books located in countries like Australia and Canada which are void of the presence of any Indigenous populations and again exclusively feature white characters.

COVER SHORT-CHANGE

This is a term we devised to describe books in which characters of colour are just featured on front covers, conveying the promise of presence within the body of the narrative, only for the reader to open the book and find that the cover is the sole place where the character is visible.

SHORT-TERM STAY

This is an extension of the idea of 'cover short-change'. It describes instances in which racially minoritised characters are introduced at the beginning of the book but are either written out very quickly or never mentioned again in the text. In the most extreme case in the 2018 submissions, a character of colour disappeared as early as page three and failed to reappear thereafter.

ETHNIC FLUIDITY

This is a term that describes instances in which the ethnicity of the illustrated character varies from spread to spread therefore making the ethnicity indistinguishable and undefinable. If, through the review process, we are unable to racially code a character then it is reasonable to assume that a young reader will find it challenging to identify the character as a character of colour, which undermines the book's capacity to reflect realities effectively.

FACELESS OR FEATURELESS

This style of illustration, in which characters' faces are featureless, is a valid artistic choice. However, it can make the processing of the books and the identification of the presence of characters of colour challenging. The nature of such an illustration style creates a homogeneity that eliminates the ability to categorise ethnicity. Such a choice undermines the validity of such titles in terms of them being recognised as an example of representative and inclusive literature, particularly if such a portrayal is the only indicator of presence of characters of colour in the book.

JASMINE DEFAULT

We acknowledge that there will be multiple reasons as to why a character may resonate with a reader and ethnicity forms only one of those reasons. That said, in the early review cycles we experienced a disproportionately high number of female characters named 'Jasmine'. The name was, in many instances, the only cue available to suggest that the character was a character of colour and therefore appeared to be the reason the book was submitted to the Reflecting Realities survey. The name is commonly used across cultures and does not necessarily denote one particular ethnic demographic group, community or culture; if this is the only cue available then we would question whether the book is truly representative. This term is a shorthand for a book where the only indicator of ethnicity is a character's name.

WALLPAPERING

'Wallpapering' is a shorthand term we developed to describe a style of illustration where the background is densely populated or at least featured a number of background characters. A repeat pattern achieved by intermittently colouring in characters either black or brown to the extent that it almost resembled a wallpaper effect, often resulted in minoritised characters blending in so much so that they became lost in the crowd. This is fine in principle if everyone is getting lost in a generic crowd but in the early cycles of this work, we had repeated incidences of books being submitted as representative of characters of colour where this was their only presence in the book – in such cases this could be interpreted as a form of relegation.

HAIR CUE

Hair cue relates to instances where the only point of reference that might suggest that the character was a character of colour was the description of their hair, specifically as either 'wavy' or 'curly'. Again, given the nature of this study, such cues alone are a tenuous and insufficient reason for submission to a survey on representation; they do not offer substantial dimensions to the characterisation in a way that would be sufficiently meaningful.

HOMOGENISED ILLUSTRATIVE STYLE

Homogenised illustrative styles that were evident in some submitted titles make it difficult to identify characters of colour, rendering the title in a number of cases as invalid for the purposes of the study and raising questions about relatability.

VACANT LANDSCAPE

This relates to titles in which the story is located in a country outside the UK in which the lack of people featured in the illustration suggests a lack of population or presence. Such spreads and titles could potentially lead a young reader to infer that such spaces are under-developed, barren or primitive.

> We have looked at our book stock and have found some very old school texts that have what I would call very stereotypical images in them that are used as dual-language books. They are written in a range of languages and then also translated into English. When we looked through them, we felt that those immediately had to come off the shelves because they portrayed stereotypical images of what families from 'other' cultures looked like. And actually, to us, these were poor representations. That's definitely an action we've taken as a result of really thinking carefully about the books we have and whether they are supporting a positive image or representation of a particular community or whether they're feeding into some kind of general stereotype.

Class teacher

The glossary of terms and this notion of being 'visibly invisible' illustrates that it is not enough to create a platform for characters of colour. Due consideration must be given to how their stories and characterisations are formulated and expressed. The value of providing a spotlight for inclusive narratives is diminished if the light reveals poorly considered, inadequate or problematic representations. These terms are intended as a tool to help to fine tune our radar when considering what makes a good-quality representative book and alert us to some of the pitfalls to look out for.

THE LIMITATIONS OF LANGUAGE AND THE IMPORTANCE OF DETERMINING THE PRESENCE OF SPECIFIC DEMOGRAPHIC GROUPS

Using broad terms such as 'characters of colour' or 'racially minoritised characters' serves a purpose in focusing our discourse, but they can be limiting in that they encompass such a broad range of communities of peoples with distinctive linguistic, cultural and historical roots. When we evaluate the specific ethnicity of the characters of colour we encounter in the books we review, it is evident that the large proportion of distinctive demographic groups are significantly under-represented. The extent of under-representation of marginalised ethnic demographic groups combined with varied quality of output means that the quality of presence when we do encounter it is all the more important.

It can be challenging to know how to integrate these principles with the foundation set out at the start of this chapter and know where to start and how to use these insights to inform our book stock curation. The simple framework in Figure 4.6 offers a means to guide your considerations when evaluating your classroom book stock. It encourages you to ensure that your classroom book corners feature stock that comprises a breadth and range of titles that normalise the presence of racially minoritised characters and in doing so counteracts erasure, redresses imbalances and challenges thinking. Any given title will embody one, some or all of these functions simultaneously. So, to diminish the burden of one book having to carry the weight of all of these expectations, we need to ensure that our book corners are stocked with a high volume of good-quality ethnically representative and inclusive literature that encompasses a breadth and range of contexts, subjects, themes, genres and writing styles. These four components offer useful markers against which to review and build your stock.

So, let's consider how these functions might translate in terms of your book stock.

CORE FRAMEWORK FOR REVIEWING HOW EFFECTIVELY BOOK STOCK REFLECTS REALITIES

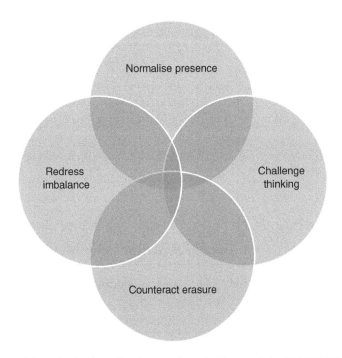

Figure 4.6   Framework for reviewing how effectively book stock reflects realities ©CLPE 2023

NORMALISING PRESENCE

When reflecting on your book stock, do you have a range of titles that mirror facets of children's linguistic, ethnic and cultural identities but in which 'otherness' is not the underpinning feature? Such titles will centre characters of colour engaging in everyday activities, having universal experiences and encountering dilemmas and challenges that are not necessarily intrinsically bound in their ethnicity. The series of picturebooks published by Alanna Max featuring the everyday exploits of siblings Lulu and Zeki is a prime example of how this might be conveyed. Each book focuses on exploring a key experience and includes titles such as *Lulu Gets a Cat, Lulu Love Flowers, Lulu's First Day, Zeki Gets a Check Up, Zeki Can Swim* and *Zeki Sleep Tight* (McQuinn and Hearson, 2019–22). The care and attention paid to the details in the spread taken from *Lulu's Sleep Over* beautifully show how such normalisation can be achieved. The delicate shaft of light emitted from the top right corner of the image bathes Lulu in light, serving as a spotlight and in doing so elevating her status. The feline trinkets tell us about her love of cats. The smattering of books piled in different corners of the room indicate that she enjoys reading. The framed photos in the background give us a sense of the important relationships in her life. Her hairstyle and the print of her dress offer a nod to her culture and heritage. The fact that she is taking the time to choose what she might wear and what she will pack indicates a healthy sense of agency. Every detail effectively works together to provide a rich, multi-dimensional portrayal that features relatable components, as well as honouring Lulu's unique individuality. Scenes like this and titles that explore such everyday occurrences with the same care and consideration and centre characters of colour in everyday narratives in this way enable a normalisation of such presence and contribute to making their presence mainstream.

Figure 4.7   *Lulu's Sleepover.* Written by Anna McQuinn, illustrations Rosalind Beardshaw, 2021

COUNTERACTING ERASURE

While normalising presence from title to title is a key starting point, this principle must necessarily extend across literary genres. Centring carefully crafted, multi-dimensional characters of colour with nuanced narrative arcs in spaces that have traditionally been populated by exclusively white casts is crucial to normalising and making their presence mainstream. Author Catherine Johnson's important body of work in the area of historical fiction in which she brings the past to life through compelling narratives and engaging protagonists of colour is a key example of this (see Bibliography). Her works span across reading ages from Key Stage 2–4 and her respect for the discipline of historical enquiry and her chosen subject matter are evident in every title. Her careful and extensive research, combined with her passion and commitment to creating well-developed, well-drawn and nuanced characters set against authentic historical backdrops, elevates both the historical subject matter and the reader. Her work has set the bar and been fundamental in laying the groundwork for the subsequent success of titles like the Scholastic Voices series. Each title in the series is set in a different period of British history which is explored through the perspective of a character of colour. These serve to fill the blank spaces that traditionally exist in this regard and help to challenge any misconceptions about the long-standing presence and relationship that racially minoritised communities have had with Britain.

CHALLENGE THINKING

Books have a crucial role to play in supporting children to broaden their knowledge base and develop their skills of critical reflection. Through exposure to information, ideas and a range of perspectives we can deepen, broaden and challenge thinking. In recent years we have seen a growing volume of output in the children's literature market that has sought to contribute to the discourse on the legacies of imperialism and support understanding of how Britain has come to be the country it is today. David Olusoga's *Black and British: A Short Essential History* (2020) and the follow-up illustrated version (2021) have been important contributions to this trend. Both titles serve as invaluable sources of information and challenge thinking by virtue of compensating for knowledge gaps that can be compounded by narrow and constrained curriculum provision. The comprehensive chronology contained within this title serves as an important means of counteracting reductive approaches to incorporating the study of Black figures, communities, movements, societies and civilisations. Books like this expand existence, timelines and contribution beyond the limiting parameters of narratives of exceptionalism, struggle, strife and subjugation. They afford greater scope for achieving a broader and more balanced learning experience and a richer more authentic history programme of study. For example, the 2014 Key Stage 2 History programme of study requires the *'study of an aspect or theme in British history that extends pupils' chronological knowledge beyond 1066'* and can be amply accommodated with the recent increasing availability of titles set across key periods of British history. These titles can be mapped out to serve as rich stimuli to inspire interesting and varied units of study, as in the example in Figure 4.8.

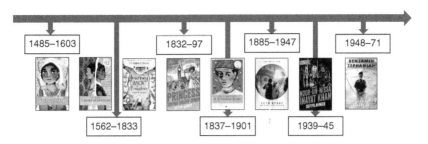

Figure 4.8   See copyright list on page xvi

REDRESS IMBALANCE

As curators of book stock, teachers of contemporary classrooms have a very different kind of challenge compared to 15 or even ten years ago. Typically, the contents of our book corners in the past have been skewed by what is available on the market, so unless you went seeking in specialist independent bookshops you tended to have quite a limited range of often imported ethnically inclusive, representative literature. The themes of that literature would have tended to either focus on the celebration of religious festivals, coverage of the American Civil Rights Movement, profiling of international icons such as Nelson Mandela, traditional tales or the study of ancient civilisations. Consequently, the thematic leaning would have swayed towards narratives of exceptionalism or struggle. The increased output being produced in the UK and abroad covering a range of subjects, themes and genres in the last five years means we are now in the position to be able to refine our book corner collections to ensure a better breadth and balance of representative titles that cover a range of lived and imaginary experiences, themes, text types and genres.

> *I think there are opportunities at times for the children to be exposed to different world views and different outlooks. But it's quite constrained and I think what was really missing here was just that representation of everyday characters, everyday storylines and opportunities for the children to make connections. I think we were really good at having those kinds of books that showcase the struggle that ethnic minorities can have. So we have, books like* The Boy at the Back of the Class *(Rauf, 2018) as part of our curriculum and titles like* Malala's Magic Pencil *(Yousafzai and Kerascoët, 2019); these were all showcased across the curriculum. I think a few years ago, people definitely got into the trap of solely using those texts and thinking that this is what it meant to be diverse and representative. So I think our children were just missing that everyday representation.*
>
> **Senior leader**

With that said, this should not be considered a matter of having to choose between one text type or another. There is absolutely a place and need for exploring narratives of struggle, as they provide insights into important eras, movements, moments and figures in the history of our humanity. However, if children only ever encounter individuals of colour in books exclusively through the lens of struggle then such restriction can endorse problematic other-ing and reinforce false hierarchies.

If you do stock titles that explore such narratives, it is essential that they are carefully researched, do the subject justice and are sensitive and thoughtful in their portrayals. A prime example of what this might look like in practice is a title such as *The Undefeated* (2020) which is an award-winning collaboration between Kwame Alexander and Kadir Nelson that celebrates the complex, painful and inspiring history of the African American community over time. The deceptively simple artistic choices conveyed in each spread offer such deep and sophisticated layers of meaning, as in the example featured in Figure 4.9. The illustrator Kadir Nelson shows the protestors arm in arm, aligned with no gaps, emphasising the wall-like strength of their unity and conviction. He has chosen to include the late iconic civil rights activist John Lewis alongside everyday men and women as well as white religious figures to show the collective commitment to the struggle and highlight the ally-ship in the movement. What is also particularly poignant is Nelson's choice to set this scene against a white background as it gives the struggle a timeless quality by creating a sense that you could plot this image at any point in our recent history and it would still continue to be relevant. This, combined with the gradual increase in font size end-ing on the words 'Black lives matter', emphasises the way this expression has echoed in the fight for justice throughout history. The book is a perfect embodiment of how to convey and explore social injustice in a way that honours the subject and doesn't patronise the young reader.

Figure 4.9   ©Kwame Alexander and Kadir Nelson

Such titles offer invaluable means of understanding ourselves, each other and world around us. They serve as a form of reconciliatory narrative – because, through their exploration of distinctive struggles and exceptional feats, these kinds of books help us to recognise, address, challenge and come to terms with the injustices of the past and understand how these events have come to shape present times. However, equal if not greater weighting must be given to normalising narratives, which are essentially books that centre characters of colour and encom-pass a breadth of themes across a range of literary genres such as adventure, mystery, science fiction, horror, comedy, fantasy and everything else in between: comedic titles that skilfully invite readers to laugh along with characters of colour, such as *Danny Chung Does Not Do*

Maths by Maisie Chan (2021), the *Planet Omar* series by Zanib Mian (2019–22), the *Cookie!* series by Konnie Huq (2019–21) and Burhana Islam's trilogy that begins with her debut title, *Mayhem Mission* (2021–3); adventure mysteries that keep readers guessing at every turn like Sharna Jackson's *High-Rise Mystery* (2019), Patrice Lawrence's *Elemental Detectives* (2022a), Serena Patel's *Anisha, Accidental Detective* series (2020–3) or Sophie Deen's *Agent Asha* titles (2020, 2022); dystopian dramas like Polly Ho-Yen's *Boy in the Tower* (2015); time-travelling adventures like Patience Agbabi's *Leap Cycle* series (2020–4); and reimagined fairy tales like Joseph Coelho's *Zombierella* (2020) or Jamila Gavin's *Blackberry Blue* (2014). Such titles broaden the realm of possibility by challenging the idea that the literary space is an exclusive domain and showcasing that instead it can and should be a place where all are welcome. Striking this balance (Figure 4.10) through what we have on offer in our book corners does the important job of counteracting erasure and marginalisation and, in doing so, not only challenges ideas about the literary space, but also creates new expectations in this regard, giving licence to young writers to be inspired to emulate this through their own creative writing endeavours.

BALANCING NARRATIVES, THEMES AND GENRES

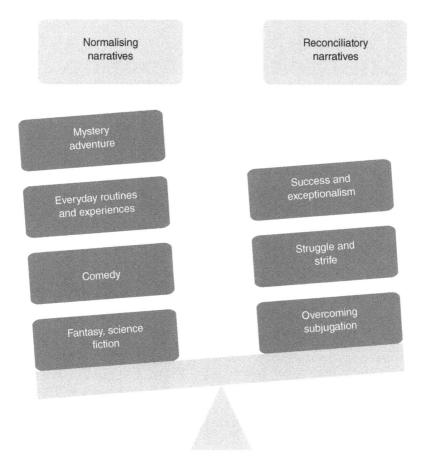

Figure 4.10   Balancing Narratives, Themes and Genres to Ensure that Book Stock Reflects Realities ©CLPE 2023

CLPE book stock review tool

		Did you identify any gaps? If so what were these?	What areas of development might be required?	General comments/ observations
What proportion of your book stock features characters of colour?	Up to 25% Up to 50% Up to 75% More than 75%			
What is the balance of representation of distinctive ethnic groups within your book stock? (*List the ethnic groups present and note the estimated percentage of presence in each instance)	*			
Normalising presence: **What proportion of your book stock features characters of colour portrayed in everyday narratives exploring universal themes that normalise and make mainstream their presence?**	Up to 25% Up to 50% Up to 75% More than 75%			
Counteracting erasure: **what proportion of your book stock centres characters of colour across all literary genres?** (**List the range of literary genres available and note the estimated percentage of presence in each instance)	**			

Figure 4.11 CLPE Reflecting Realities Book Stock Review Tool ©CLPE 2023

CLPE book stock review tool

	Picturebooks	Fiction (short stories, novels, illustrated novels)	Non-fiction	Poetry
Approximately how many of each text type do you have in your class book stock?	0–10 10–25 25–40 40–55 55–70 More than 70 **(circle as appropriate)**	0–10 10–25 25–40 40–55 55–70 More than 70 **(circle as appropriate)**	0–10 10–25 25–40 40–55 55–70 More than 70 **(circle as appropriate)**	0–10 10–25 25–40 40–55 55–70 More than 70 **(circle as appropriate)**
What percentage of your class book stock is comprised of …	Up to 25% Up to 50% Up to 75% More than 75% **(circle as appropriate)**	Up to 25% Up to 50% Up to 75% More than 75% **(circle as appropriate)**	Up to 25% Up to 50% Up to 75% More than 75% **(circle as appropriate)**	Up to 25% Up to 50% Up to 75% More than 75% **(circle as appropriate)**
Approximately how many of the books within each text type in your stock were published in the last 5 years?				
Approximately how many of the books within each text type in your stock are written by an author of colour?				
What observations might you draw about the breadth and balance of representation of authors of colour in your book stock for each category?				

(Continued)

(Continued)

	Note the literary genres available in your stock and identify any gaps:	Note the non-fiction genres available in your stock and identify any gaps:	
Do you have a breadth and range of literary genres within your fiction and non-fiction stock?			
Do characters of colour feature across the range of literary genres within your fiction and non-fiction stock?			
Do you have a breadth and range of coverage of themes and topics within each text type in your existing stock?			
Are the themes and topics explored in titles featuring characters of colour varied, covering subject matter in which ethnicity is at times pertinent and in other instances incidental?			
Of the books in each text type category that feature a main character, what proportion of these main characters is a character of colour?	Up to 25% Up to 50% Up to 75% More than 75% (circle as appropriate)	Up to 25% Up to 50% Up to 75% More than 75% (circle as appropriate)	Up to 25% Up to 50% Up to 75% More than 75% (circle as appropriate)

How many of the books in each text type category in your stock feature any characters of colour?	Up to 25% Up to 50% Up to 75% More than 75% **(circle as appropriate)**	Up to 25% Up to 50% Up to 75% More than 75% **(circle as appropriate)**	Up to 25% Up to 50% Up to 75% More than 75% **(circle as appropriate)**	Up to 25% Up to 50% Up to 75% More than 75% **(circle as appropriate)**
Note which ethnic groups are represented in the casts of characters within each text type				
What observations can you draw from this about the breadth and balance of representation of characters of colour in your book stock for each text type?				
What are your key priorities following this review of your book stock for each text type?				
Do you anticipate any challenges in addressing these priorities? What are these and how might you overcome them?				

Figure 4.12 CLPE Reflecting Realities Book Stock Review Tool ©CLPE 2023

With these ideals in mind, the first step of reviewing book stock should involve determining the nature and extent of the presence of characters of colour. Take the time to browse your existing stock and use the table in Figure 4.11 to guide your considerations about the extent to which the titles meet these requirements and in doing so support children from racially minoritised backgrounds to derive connection while broadening the knowledge base and associations for all readers regardless of their background.

Having considered the extent of presence to enable connection and representation in a broad sense, create a table like the example shown in 4.12 to delve a little deeper.

What did this exercise reveal? What observations can you draw from your responses about the breadth and balance of representation of characters of colour in your stock? How varied is the presence? What is the quality of the presence? If your existing stock scored low in terms of the extent and quality of its inclusivity, this may very well be because you haven't been able to purchase new stock. This may mean your book corner is made up of titles published some time ago and until quite recently the publishing output of children's literature was not particularly representative. You may have identified healthy presence in some text types but less so in others.

Using these tools to support the evaluation of your classroom book stock will undoubtedly highlight both areas of strength and areas for development. The gaps will vary from text type to text type and from year group to year group. Budgetary constraints might hinder the capacity to remedy any identified gaps in the short term, which is why it is important that these stock audits form the basis of a starting point in planning the nature and scope of investment required. This can then be factored into short-, interim and long-term budgetary allocations, fundraising initiatives or funding applications to enable your school to invest in building stock over time. Such investment should be viewed as a core entitlement for your entire school community because, through such investment, you will improve stock provision, allowing for a richer breadth of choice that will enrich the reading diet, elevate the literacy programmes of study and enhance your school's reading culture and community.

CHAPTER 5

DEVELOPING AN INCLUSIVE READING CULTURE IN THE CLASSROOM

> Roald Dahl's *Boy* had a lasting impact. It was probably the first autobiography I'd read and I read it multiple times. I think I was inspired by how seemingly ordinary events were made extraordinary. It's genius. Also, Meera Syal's *Anita and Me*. It was the first book I saw myself in. Words cannot express how important that book was in my house. I remember staring at the cover for ages. I couldn't believe there was a picture of a South Asian girl on the front cover! Not only that but it was a story about a South Asian, working class girl from the Black Country. I totally saw myself in that book and my mind was blown.
>
> Manjeet Mann

Manjeet Mann is a multi-award-winning children's author, actress, playwright and screenwriter. Her debut YA novel *Run Rebel* (Penguin, 2020) was shortlisted for the Carnegie Medal 2021 and the CLiPPA and won the CILIP Carnegie Shadowers' Choice Award, the UKLA Award, Diverse Book Award and Sheffield Children's Book Award. It was also a *Guardian* best book of 2020. Her second novel *The Crossing* (Penguin, 2021) won the Costa Children's Book Award and UKLA Award and was shortlisted for the CLiPPA. In 2022 her first picture book, *Small's Big Dreams*, illustrated by Amanda Quartey, was published by HarperCollins. Manjeet is also the founder of Run the World, a not-for-profit that uses sport and theatre as a means to empower women and girls.

The quote here is from Manjeet's blog about *Small's Big Dreams*, written for CLPE in 2022.

Find out more:

In the previous chapter we spent time assessing how representative and inclusive our current book stock is. To optimise the value and impact of that book stock it is important to next consider how texts are utilised and positioned within our programmes of study and provision.

We will encourage you to build on your assessment of your book provision by reflecting on how this stock contributes to a wider set of considerations which will help you develop an inclusive reading culture. This will include the decisions we make about our English curriculum and the texts that we study as part of that curriculum. We'll think about how we can construct a reading spine that supports us to develop an inclusive approach but also enables us to make sense of statutory requirements and literary canons.

There are many questions we need to ask ourselves when we are defining and creating the reading culture in our school. This culture should be shaped by a collective vision and informed by a considered pedagogical foundation that translates into thoughtfully implemented practices, routines and provision.

What is the reading culture in our setting? How has it been cultivated? Who has been involved in determining and shaping it? How effective is it in nurturing competent and confident readers who enjoy reading and excel at it? How you answer these questions will provide indications about how well established and impactful your school's reading culture is.

What is your school's vision? Do all members of your school community share this vision and feel invested? What theories and principles underpin your pedagogical foundation? Is there a staff consensus and collective buy-in of these principles? Do staff feel confident in their understanding and application of these principles as part of their everyday practice? What opportunity is there to routinely review and refine this, both individually and collectively? We could consider what each component involved in creating a reading culture means to us as professionals, what it looks like in our current settings and evaluate what works and what could work better.

However, as the focus of this book is to determine the value and means of reflecting realities in the classroom and the use of representative literature, let's contain our considerations to thinking about how the text choices we make contribute to this culture. Let's work on the assumption that our current setting takes a book-centred approach to the teaching of literacy and that children encounter quality literature across all areas of study.

To expand further, this baseline assumes that the defining components of high-quality book provision include titles that feature:

- wide-ranging themes
- compelling subject matter
- rich language
- varied writing styles
- creative story-telling with strong narrative arcs
- multi-dimensional characters
- sophisticated inter-play with words and images in illustrated titles
- innovative and engaging formats.

We also assume the reading materials on offer through the literacy provision and wider programmes of study will form the basis of every child's reading diet and that there will be ample opportunity for children to meaningfully engage with such titles.

The reading materials we offer contribute to the reading culture by conveying the scope of what the act of reading has to offer. The broader the range of text types and content, the wider the scope for appreciating the purposes and gains that reading can provide. It also plays an important part of defining children's understanding and expectations of the literary space.

Every book shared in your classroom – be it through the book corner, during a story time session, as a focus for study or recommendation – serves as a form of endorsement. It is therefore important to consider how these endorsements might be perceived and how they might influence children's impressions and appreciation of books as well as their engagement with texts and subsequent choices. For example, if we disproportionately draw on one text type, or the same titles year on year or lean on the works of a narrow range of authors, this won't give children a true picture of what is available in the wider 'book world' and could well give the impression to children that we, the adults, attribute greater value towards some text types over others. CLPE's *Power of Pictures* (Anders et al., 2021) programme, for example, has been instrumental in challenging ideas about the value of picturebooks for learners of all ages. Through this work we have encountered perceptions from children and adults alike that picturebooks are considered more appropriate for Early Years Foundation Stage (EYFS) and Key Stage 1 classrooms. This misconception limits opportunities for older children to encounter the extensive range of engaging, thought-provoking, sophisticated picturebooks that have the potential to deepen, elevate and enrich their reading experiences as well as offer important challenge to support their reading development.

MEETING NATIONAL EXPECTATIONS

The current English National Curriculum published in 2014 requires schools in England to ensure that children encounter a wide range and breadth of books that *feed [their] imagination and open up a treasure-house of wonder and joy for curious young minds'* during the primary phase of their schooling. The Key Stage 1 (5–7) and 2 (7–11) English Programmes of Study comment that through reading, *'pupils have a chance to develop culturally, emotionally, intellectually, socially and spiritually'* and asserts that, *'all pupils must be encouraged to read widely across both fiction and non-fiction to develop their knowledge of themselves and the world in which they live, to establish an appreciation and love of reading, and to gain knowledge across the curriculum'*. Given the complex, varied and layered requirements that our text choices need to fulfil to engage, challenge and inspire our children, it's worth considering how consistently children encounter books that not only serve as tools to support the development of their reading skills, but also stimulate their cultural, intellectual, social and spiritual capacities. While the National Curriculum does not prescribe specific titles, it does indicate that this range should at the very least include the text types detailed in the table in Figure 5.1.

The curriculum does not provide definitions of these text types or guidance regarding selection. Instead, it is down to us to use our professional judgement to select titles that fulfil this wide and sophisticated set of criteria in a way that ensures progression in the demands of the text as the children move through the year groups and key stages. Many of us add another layer of challenge by also attempting to choose books that cover subject matter that offers the scope to support cross-curricular study. We might choose a text set in a particular historical era, for example, enabling the text to perform double duty in both our English and history lessons. This allows children to spend more time in this distinctive world and draw on the fictional account for context and relatability which supports them in making the leap in their appreciation of a distant period and abstract world.

National Curriculum English Programme of Study Key Stage 1	National Curriculum English Programme of Study Key Stage 2
Contemporary and classic poetry Key stories Fairy stories Traditional tales Non-fiction	Modern fiction and fiction from our literary heritage Fairy stories Traditional stories Myths and legends Non-fiction Reference books Textbooks Dictionaries Poetry Plays Books from other cultures and traditions

Figure 5.1   Summary of Text Types featured in the National Curriculum 2014 ©CLPE 2023

With these multiple factors in mind, take a moment to reflect on the texts that have formed the basis of your most recent year of teaching. Select the grid in either Figure 5.2 or 5.3 that matches the phase in which you teach and create a table to note the texts that have formed the basis of your core literacy teaching, placing them in the column that best describes the text.

Key Stage 1				
Contemporary and classic poetry	Key stories	Fairy stories	Traditional tales	Non-fiction

Figure 5.2   Key Stage 1 Text Review Grid ©CLPE 2023

Key Stage 2					
Fiction • **Modern fiction** • **Fiction from our literary heritage**	**Fairy stories** **Traditional stories** **Myths and legends**	**Non-fiction** **Reference books** **Textbooks** **Dictionaries**	**Poetry**	**Plays**	**Books from other cultures and traditions**

Figure 5.3   Key Stage 1 Text Review Grid ©CLPE 2023

Having completed this exercise, take a moment to reflect on the titles in your grid. How satisfied are you that they fulfil the wider aspirations set out in the National Curriculum?

TAKE TiME TO CONSiDER

Are some text types disproportionately under- or over-represented? How varied is the subject and thematic matter?

Now consider the casting. How many of your titles feature a main character of colour? How many of the books in your grid feature any characters of colour? Are the characters of colour featured well-crafted, multi-dimensional and authentically depicted individuals? Do they have agency? Do they meaningfully contribute to the narrative? How varied are the portrayals across the titles? How wide-ranging is the demographic make-up of the characters of colour featured within and across the titles? Note your reflections on or around your grid. Consider what the implications might be for your text choices moving forward. For some of us it will be a case of maintaining the balance we have established and replenishing and adapting year-group lists to respond to the ever-growing choices available to us to keep the range fresh and interesting. In other instances, we might have identified areas that need development and investment.

To help us further consider how the texts we choose to centre might influence the reading culture of our settings, take a moment to review the pre-populated grids in Figures 5.4 and 5.5 which feature a sample of texts that satisfy the statutory requirements. The texts in these grids are titles that would typically have been found in book corners and formed the basis of units of study around the time we were seeking funding to review children's

Contemporary and classic poetry	Key stories	Sample of titles, Key Stage 1		Non-fiction
		Fairy stories	Traditional tales	
The Owl and the Pussy Cat (author: Edward Lear, illustrator: Ian Beck, publisher: Corgi)	*We're Going on a Bear Hunt* (author: Michael Rosen, illustrator: Helen Oxenbury, publisher: Walker)	*The Gingerbread Man* (illustrator: Estelle Corke, publisher: Child's Play)	*Goldilocks and Just the One Bear* (author/illustrator: Leigh Hodgkinson, publisher: Nosy Crow)	*Major Glad, Major Dizzy* (author: Jan Oke, photographer: Ian Nolan, publisher: Little Knowall)
Please Mrs Butler (author: Allan Ahlberg, publisher: Puffin)	*The Tiger who came to Tea* (author/ illustrator: Judith Kerr, publisher: Harper Collins)	*The Billy Goats Gruff* (illustrator: Alison Edgson, publisher: Child's Play)	*The Boy Who Cried Wolf* (illustrator: Jess Stockham, publisher: Child's Play)	*The Great Fire of London: An Illustrated History of the Great Fire of 1666* (author: Emma Adams, illustrator: James Weston Lewis, publisher: Wren and Rook)
Revolting Rhymes (author: Roald Dahl, illustrator: Quentin Blake, publisher: Puffin)	*The Gruffalo* (author: Julia Donaldson, illustrator: Axel Scheffler, publisher: Macmillan)	*Jack and the Beanstalk* (author: Stephen Tucker, illustrator: Nick Sharratt, publisher: Macmillan)	*The True Story of the Three Little Pigs* (author: Jon Scieszka, illustrator: Lane Smith, publisher: Puffin)	*Florence Nightingale* (author/illustrator: Demi, publisher: Henry Holt and Co.)

Figure 5.4 Sample Key Stage 1 Text Grid ©CLPE 2023

publishing output in 2016. They feature a range of contemporary classics and award-winning titles with subject matter, themes and literary features that would engage children and support them at different stages of literacy development while inspiring a range of learning opportunities. Starting with the Key Stage 1 table, what do you notice about the cast of characters featured? Within this sample, can you identify any characters of colour?

If you're struggling to do so it's because aside from the one token character on the front cover of the 2013 edition of Allan Ahlberg's *Please Mrs Butler*, there aren't any. If this sample were to form the sole basis of a child's core literacy learning over the course of their time in Key Stage 1, what impression might this convey? What might it suggest about who does and doesn't belong in the literary space?

Holding onto these thoughts, let's turn our attentions to the Key Stage 2 sample. Similarly, this is a varied selection of firm favourites of tried and tested titles that fulfil wide-ranging teaching requirements. As with the previous sample, take the time to identify any titles featuring characters of colour. What do you notice?

What you might have identified is that, although we might see more presence compared to the Key Stage 1 grid, this tends to be in titles set in the past through the study of ancient civilisations, traditional tales or books from other cultures. This can mean that children potentially go through the entire primary phase of their education and not encounter books that are written by authors of colour or feature characters of colour or at best only encounter them in genres that render them relics of the past or othered as wise sages with little relatability or relevance to contemporary British society.

It is important to make clear that the critique is not of the titles featured in the tables. On the contrary they are sound, high-quality books that offer much value and great opportunities for rich dialogue and learning. They should absolutely form part of the book corner and reading experiences. The point of the critique is in relation to how limiting books we share with children to texts that do not feature characters of colour can skew their experience and impressions of what literature can offer and who is entitled to occupy the literary space.

The books we choose to share, recommend, stock and integrate into our curriculum convey to our children what is valid and valued in the literary space. If these choices result in the absence or marginalisation of characters of colour, we can potentially reinforce the erasure and problematic degradation of communities of colour in other spheres of society. The legitimisation of such erasure defines not only our reading culture, but also our wider learning culture.

What we found in a very short time span is that ever since we've started introducing these books as part of our core curriculum, the children are now able to relate to texts and narratives much more easily. We have seen that they have become much more open in their discussions and we can see that children have a real sense of pride in their heritage as well and they're much more eager to share.

Class teacher

For some children in the English schooling system, their first encounter with characters of colour will be in secondary school. Texts featuring characters of colour in this phase of schooling have come under scrutiny in recent times through important advocacy (Chantiluke et al., 2021) calling for review and remedy. Viewing the reading diet across key stages from the primary phase into secondary schooling in this way highlights the fact that a child could potentially go

Key Stage 2

Fiction • Modern Fiction • Fiction from our Literary Heritage	Fairy Stories Traditional Stories Myths and Legends	Non–fiction Reference Books Textbooks Dictionaries	Poetry	Plays	Books from other Cultures and Traditions
Matilda (author: Roald Dahl, publisher: Penguin) *Private Peaceful* (author: Michael Morpurgo, publisher: HarperCollins) *Tom's Midnight Garden* (author: Phillipa Pearce, publisher: OUP)	*Hansel and Gretel* (author/illustrator: Anthony Browne, publisher: Walker) *Red and the City* (author/ illustrator: Marie Voigt, publisher: OUP) *Adventures of Odysseus* (author: Hugh Lupton, illustrator: Christina Balit, publisher: Barefoot)	*So You Think You've Got It Bad? A Kid's Life in Ancient Egypt* (author: Chae Strathie, illustrator: Marisa Morea, publisher: Nosy Crow) *UG: Boy Genius of the Stone Age and His Search for Soft Trousers* (author/illustrator: Raymond Briggs, publisher: Puffin) *NGK Everything Vikings: All the Incredible Facts and Fierce Fun You Can Plunder* (National Geographic Kids)	*Poetry Pie* (author: Roger McGough, publisher: Puffin) *Mustard, Custard, Grumble Belly and Gravy* (author: Michael Rosen, illustrator: Quentin Blake, publisher: Bloomsbury) *The Highwayman* (author: Alfred Noyes, illustrator: Charles Keeping, publisher: OUP)	*Romeo and Juliet* (author: William Shakespeare, Retold by Andrew Matthews, illustrator: Tony Ross, publisher: Orchard) *Macbeth* (author: William Shakespeare, Retold by Andrew Matthews, illustrator: Tony Ross, publisher: Tony Ross)	*Fly, Eagle, Fly! An African Tale* (author: Christopher Gregorowski, illustrator: Niki Daly, publisher: Scribner) *Seasons of Splendour: Tales, Myths and Legends of India* (author: Madhur Jaffrey, illustrator: Michael Foreman, publisher: Puffin) *Beowulf* (author: Michael Morpurgo, illustrator: Michael Foreman, publisher: Walker)

Figure 5.5 Sample Key Stage 2 Text Grid ©CLPE 20233

through the education system barely encountering characters of colour in Key Stage 1, to then only encounter them on the margins in Key Stage 2 and, finally, only experience them in challenging contexts confined to narratives of struggle, subjugation or strife in Key Stage 3. This journey through literature determined by the text choices we make illustrates how misconceptions about the literary landscape and the world beyond the page can be shaped. It is important to think about the impact this might have on a young learner's sense of self and outlook and how this might compound toxic messaging received from wider channels. If the authorship and content of the school reading diet excludes the global majority and reinforces their marginalisation this perpetuates false hierarchies that can potentially diminish the self-worth of minoritised children. It can also skew impressions of the literary space and compromise the opportunity for all children to engage with the wealth of literary greatness that spans across the breadth of cultures and communities that make up our classrooms and our world.

Determining whether a text features a character of colour as a central cast member should really mark the beginning of a series of questions because presence alone is not sufficient. We need to consider: what is the extent and nature of this presence? Are the portrayals of these characters on balance meaningful and high quality? Do the characters of colour feature in a range of text types, genres and books that explore a variation of subject matter and themes? Considerations regarding the extent, nature and quality of presence of characters of colour can help to contribute towards our considerations about how texts have the potential to shape thinking. This is because, through considering how varied, balanced and meaningful the portrayals of characters of colour are, we are also determining how the texts we use support children along their journey towards becoming literate and critically reflective.

At the core of this questioning, we are seeking to determine how we meaningfully draw on literature to support children in developing a critical lens. This criticality is what elevates reading from the functionality of lifting words from a page and deciphering meaning towards the more sophisticated endeavour of critically engaging with the substance. This is key because we don't want our children just to consume literature with indifference; we want them to be critically reflective in their engagement.

In order to support children to critically engage with books, we need to develop critical frameworks to mediate discussions and develop critically reflective readers. A good way to lay the foundation would be to adopt Aidan Chambers' 'Tell Me' grid (Chambers, 2011) which gives children the licence to have and express an opinion about what they've read. The grid invites children to share their enthusiasms, in terms of what they both do and don't like about what they've read. They are encouraged to draw connections with personal experiences and wider associations in other texts, media and materials they may have encountered.

Likes	Dislikes
Patterns/connections	Questions

Figure 5.6 ©CLPE 2023

Question framework to support critical reflection with texts

1. What do we learn about the world of the story?	2. What do we know for sure?	3. What do we think we know?
4. What does this make us think?	5. How does this make us feel?	6. Why might the author have chosen to tell this story?
7. Is this a story that needed to be told? Why/why not?	8. From whose perspective is the story told? How does this influence our views and experience of the book? How might this have differed if it were written from an alternative perspective?	9. What themes does the story explore? Are these themes sensitively and effectively explored?
10. Have we encountered similar characters, storylines or themes in other books or films?	11. How were they similar or different? Which portrayal did you prefer and why?	12. Would you recommend this book? Why? Why not?

Figure 5.7 Question Framework to support Critical Reflection ©CLPE 2023

The initial responses collected from these questions can be built upon by eliciting deeper responses to the text using prompts such as those suggested in the reader response framework provided in Figure 5.7. This offers one way in which to develop the discourse, encouraging readers to question their impressions and thinking.

Open-ended prompts like the examples in the grids provided will support readers to get under the skin of the text and contemplate the thoughts and feelings it evokes and the impact it has. This will help them to build and refine their critical engagement with texts over time and broaden their thinking about the impact of the artistic and multi-media content they consume through making intertextual links. To facilitate such rich dialogue, we need to ensure that the texts we draw on are appropriately varied in their content and challenge to enable the process of discourse and engagement summarised in Figure 5.8

TEXT SELECTION CRITERIA TO SUPPORT CRITICAL REFLECTION

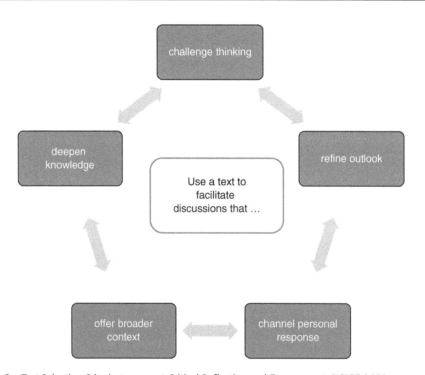

Figure 5.8   Text Selection Criteria to support Critical Reflection and Engagement ©CLPE 2023

TEXT COMPLEXITY AND CLASSICS

Our professional judgement regarding the components of text complexity and how these might support the development of criticality and progression in reading comprehension is informed by many things. As teachers, we undergo a constant cycle of trial and error that allows us to develop experience of how responsive children have been and an appreciation of what has and hasn't worked. This enables us to adapt and refine our practices and form a body of reference and a repertoire of texts to draw upon. We are also guided by our peers, leadership team, school pedagogical stance, wider reading, research and educational policy and guidance.

Although statutory guidance has not specified titles for study in the primary phase, various initiatives and policy guidance have, in the last decade, expressed a preference towards certain text types. The Ofsted *Research Review Series: English*, July 2022, stated that,

> *The national curriculum requires that reading instruction, through each key stage, should prepare pupils ultimately to read more complex texts, for example 'to read and appreciate the depth and power of the English literary heritage'. Variation in text complexity affects pupils' reading comprehension. Therefore, pupils of all ages need to be taught a curriculum that will allow them to comprehend increasingly complex texts.*

When determining the complexity level of a text to support critical reflection, we might presume that longer, denser texts such as 'classics' represent the peak that we need to aspire to. There has been a great deal written about English heritage texts or classics both in terms of how we define them and with regard to their merits and shortcomings.

Darren Chetty and Karen Sands-O'Connor address this as part of their regular *Books for Keeps* column (2020):

> *The idea that it is necessary to 'drive engagement' with the classics is not new, and not exclusive to the publishing industry. In children's literature scholarship, education and library journals, and even debates in parliament, the concern over what to do about 'classic' literature has raged over the last century. It is a debate that often pits form against content, with those in favour of keeping classics in print arguing that a good story should trump a few lapses into racist (or sexist, or homophobic, or ableist) stereotypes, especially because 'people thought differently back then'.*

It is important to consider how to respond to this tension reasonably and ethically. It is possible to choose to select contemporary classics that have the literary hallmarks of a classic without the racist or prejudicial content in place of titles written in the more distant past. Contemporary works such as Catherine Johnson's *Sawbones* (2013) or her award-winning title *Freedom* (2018), as well as S.F. Said's award-winning titles *Varjak Paw* (2014) and his most recent epic novel *Tyger* (2022) all showcase the literary finesse and story-telling mastery that would make for a rich reading experience. Each of these titles provides a substantial basis for literary study; they will stand the test of time and be more than worthy of the 'classic' label without being laced with problematic representations or tropes. With that said, advocating for the study of titles of contemporary creatives doesn't necessarily exclude the opportunity for teachers to incorporate classics from a bygone era. It doesn't have to be a case of either/or. If the latter is something we choose to do or is chosen for us within our setting, then it is important to consider how we mediate such titles. To help determine how we might go about this let's take Frances Hodgson Burnett's *The Secret Garden* as an example. First published in

1911, it has enjoyed a long shelf life with numerous film adaptations and multiple re-editions. In the ten-year period between 2011 and 2021 alone there were eight new re-editions in the UK, almost amounting to one new edition a year. This rate and frequency of reproduction is due to the lapse of copyright of titles published past a certain time frame which makes republishing classic titles a very cost-efficient and -effective exercise for publishers. The surplus often low-cost availability of such titles combined with policy and guidance that encourages engagement with these texts increases the likelihood that titles like these will feature as part of the Year 6 literacy programme of study.

In the fifth Reflecting Realities survey, we found that only 4 per cent of main cast characters featured in the 2021 output were of South Asian heritage. This means that although there is a steady growing amount of presence with regard to this demographic, children still have very few opportunities to encounter South Asian characters in the books they read. This places quite a heavy burden on the books that do feature such presence to convey high-quality, balanced portrayals. This low level of presence will naturally have a bearing on the book stock provision. Typically, if we have any South Asian presence in English programmes of study in the primary phase, this tends to comprise of a traditional tale set in India in the Early Years, a religious-based narrative recounting the story of Rama and Sita in Key Stage 1, for example, and a classic title like *The Jungle Book* or *The Secret Garden* in Key Stage 2. It is worth considering what these narratives and text types offer in terms of representation and what might be inferred from these specific portrayals. Furthermore, what kind of coverage and variations do these representations provide and what might be some of the limitations of this reading spine? What's missing and how do we supplement the reading diet to counteract this? If we were to heed the Ofsted guidance and decided to make *The Secret Garden* a set text in Year 6, what kind of groundwork would be necessary to ensure that children were equipped to critically engage with the text?

The portrayal of the very few South Asian characters featured in *The Secret Garden* is deeply problematic in a number of ways. The young protagonist Mary Lennox serves as a metaphor of the empire and as such her interactions with and disdain for the people who serve her provide the reader with glimpses into the essence of this regime. With thoughtfully planned and sensitive mediation the study of a text like this can offer the opportunity to critically evaluate the consequences of imperialism and better understand how the past has shaped contemporary Britain. Such study can go beyond literacy lessons to span across programmes of study to incorporate history, geography and PSHE. However, given the racist and derogatory depictions of the South Asian characters within this title, it is imperative that this is not the only title featuring South Asian characters that children come across as part of the primary phase of their schooling. If we are to study this text in Year 6 then we have to think about how the texts that children experience before this prepare them for this encounter. We need to ensure that we develop a reading spine that features a rich and varied range of portrayals of South Asian characters. Children need to encounter stories of individuals and communities from across the countries that make up this part of the world as well diasporic-centred narratives. The themes and genres should range from books featuring simple everyday relatable occurrences and universal dilemmas to fast-paced adventure mysteries, rib-tickling comedies, futuristic science fiction, fantasy and more. Young readers should experience the rich literary heritage of this part of the world as well as access books that build their knowledge of the historical, socio-political, economic and cultural facets of this region, understanding the relationship within and across countries across the continent and their relationship with Britain and other parts of the world. The graphic in Figure 5.9 sets out what a reading spine like this might look like. Enabling access to such breadth would allow the children to build a body of knowledge and understanding that would better equip them to approach *The Secret Garden* with the necessary level of criticality.

The sample of titles that make up the reading spine in Figure 5.9 exemplifies how we might build a body of stock that ensures children meet a breadth of representative and inclusive titles of one ethnic demographic category that comprises a range of sub-demographic groups. This exercise could and should be repeated to ensure the same opportunity for representation across racially minoritised demographic groups. It is a valuable exercise in general and particularly if we are thinking about teaching classic titles from other eras. This will enable all children to not only feel affirmed and seen but also to support the development of their knowledge and understanding of the wider world and expand their outlook.

By carefully curating reading spines, literacy units and book corners to feature high-quality inclusive and representative literature we determine the reading diets of our children and by extension the reading culture of our classrooms. The exposure to quality texts that reflect realities alongside the opportunity to exercise and develop their skills of reader response and critical reflection will support children to become confident, well-read individuals with the capacity to engage with the texts that they meet with a depth of criticality and sophistication that will be fundamental in supporting them along their academic journey. Through this deeper, more sophisticated level of engagement we shift children's relationship with reading and how they identify as readers. It becomes something they are driven to do, something that they are enthused about. It gives them key transferable skills that will raise their cognition, competency and confidence in other areas of learning. It will strengthen how they perceive themselves as learners and it sets them on the path towards becoming lifelong readers. If these fundamental gains ripple across our class of learners, we in effect have established a community of readers which in turn elevates and enriches the reading culture.

This programme has allowed me to become more of a reflective teacher and consider how children like to learn. Children have become better readers and writers but they have also enjoyed the process, always looking forward to turning the page or chapter.

Class teacher

Model reading spine that builds foundation of affirmation, knowledge base and criticality

Texts that affirm children's sense of self and broaden outlook	Texts that build knowledge base and develop reader response	Texts that encompass a range of genres and themes	Texts that explore complex themes and content	Texts set in other eras
Many Colors of Harpreet Singh (author: Supriya Kelkar, illustrator: Alea Marley, publisher: Sterling Children's)	*Pattan's Pumpkin: An Indian Flood Story* (author: Chitra Soundar, illustrator: Frané Lessac publisher: Otter–Barry)	*Tales from India* (author: Bali Rai, publisher: Puffin)	*Ajay and the Mumbai Sun* (author: Varsha Shah, illustrator: Sonia Albert, publisher: Chicken House)	*Princess Sophia Duleep Singh* (author: Sufiya Ahmed, publisher: Scholastic)
Holi Hai! (author: Chitra Soundar, illustrator: Darshika Varma, publisher: Global Publisher Services)	*Incredible India, Incredible India* (author: Jasbinder Bilan, illustrator: Nina Chakrabarti, publisher: Walker)	*Stories for South Asian Supergirls* (author: Raj Kaur Khaira, publisher: Puffin)	*City of Stolen Magic* (author: Nazneen Ahmed Pathak, publisher: Puffin)	*Noor Inayat Khan* (author: Sufiya Ahmed, publisher: Scholastic.
Sona Sharma, Very Best Big Sister (author: Chitra Soundar, illustrator: Jen Khatun, publisher: Walker)		*Ahimsa* (author: Supriya Kelkar, publisher: Tu)	*Asha and the Spirit Bird* (author: Jasbinder Bilan, publisher: Chicken House)	*Now or Never: A Dunkirk Story (Voices #1)* (author: Bali Rai, publisher: Scholastic)
Nikhil and Jay Save the Day (author: Chitra Soundar, illustrator: Soofiya, publisher: Otter–Barry)	*Twenty-Two Cents: Muhammad Yunus and the Village Bank* (author: Paula Yoo, illustrator: Jamel Akib, publisher: Lee and Low)	*Amira and Hamza: The War to Save the Worlds* (author: Samira Ahmed, publisher: Little Brown)		*Torn Apart – The Partition of India, 1947* (author: Swapna Haddow, publisher: Scholastic)
Accidental Trouble Magnet: Book 1 (Planet Omar) (author: Zanib Mian, illustrator: Nasaya Mafaridik, publisher: Hodder)				
Anisha, Accidental Detective (author: Serena Patel, illustrator: Emma McCann, publisher: Usborne)				
Ruby Ali's Mission Break Up (author: Sufiya Ahmed, illustrator: Parwinder Singh publisher: Bloomsbury)				

Figure 5.9 ©CLPE 2023

CHAPTER 6

DEFINING AND DEVELOPING WRITER IDENTITY: SUPPORTING LEARNERS TO EXPRESS THEMSELVES THROUGH WRITING AND NURTURING THEIR AUTHORIAL VOICE

> To me, reflecting realities means that the services and products surrounding us, which we use or consume on a daily basis, including the packaging and advertising of those, should match the breadth of diversity within our society. I believe that if these usual things we encounter in our everyday lives, present and celebrate people's difference, by osmosis we will become more accepting and inclusive as individuals. Conversely, if all we see is one paradigm then that becomes the accepted norm, whether it's a true reflection or not, and things that don't fit into that model start to become viewed as undesirable. For a long time, my work was a result of this unconscious shaping, in that for longer than I care to admit, I pretty much only drew white people, despite being mixed race. I didn't question it, and didn't see a problem with it.
>
> Perhaps had there been books readily available that pictured a protagonist or even a sidekick of colour, things may have been different.
>
> Lucy Farfort

Lucy Farfort is a British illustrator who won the Faber Children's inaugural FAB Prize for illustration competition in 2017. She has illustrated a range of children's picturebooks and she was the illustrator of the 2019 Reflecting Realities Report. Lucy's first solo picturebook *In Our Hands* (Tate, 2022) was a key text on the Reflecting Realities in the Classroom project and the 2023 CLPE whole school unit.

The quote here is from Lucy's blog 'What Does Reflecting Realities Mean To You?', written for CLPE in 2020.

Find out more:

THE READER IN THE WRITER

In previous chapters we considered the components that form the basis of a child's reader identity and the crucial role that inclusive literature can play in helping to shape this identity. Cultivating positive reader identities and a strong reading community and culture not only supports children's development as readers but also forms part of the necessary foundation for supporting their growth as writers.

Reading and writing are two distinctive acts that each require a specific set of core knowledge and skills. Having their distinctiveness inform our approach to the teaching of reading and writing is useful and necessary to an extent. However, if the two areas of learning are too rigidly demarcated, this can potentially mask their interconnectedness and limit the scope for children to utilise this inter-relatedness to deepen their understanding and development of these core skills.

Our reading experiences and competency are instrumental in fuelling our writing capacity. Establishing and developing a sense of writer identity is an ever-evolving process in the formative phases of a child's learning journey. Supporting children through this crucially requires an understanding and appreciation of the inter-relationship between reading and writing. *The Reader in the Writer* (Barrs and Cork, 2001) is the title of one of CLPE's most influential publications. It played a key part in supporting our understanding of the role of quality literature in deepening reader response and informing children's appreciation of writing facilitated through the use of creative teaching approaches. This learning formed the basis of the design and content of CLPE's flagship Power of Reading course which has sat at the heart of our learning programme since its publication.

The Power of Reading defines the CLPE ethos and approach to teaching literacy and, through the consistently positive outcomes achieved by participating schools, exemplifies that one of the many and core powers of reading is its capacity to develop our appreciation for good writing. The work of nurturing the reader that sits within every writer therefore not only makes children confident and engaged readers but also makes them better and considered writers.

In the first instance, it is important for children to access reading materials that resonate with them in some way, be it the content, subject matter, themes, cast of characters, language, writing style, illustrations, design, or aesthetic. As we have said elsewhere in this book, children are more likely to be drawn to texts that they connect with and this connection is also more likely to support sustained interest.

The next layer of attending to the reader in the writer involves considering the quality and range of the writing they are exposed to. If we want children to appreciate how to use written language effectively to communicate ideas, create impressions, paint pictures with words and evoke feelings through the appropriate use of varied language choices, tone and pace they need to encounter and be immersed in a wide variety of texts. The immersion and meaningful engagement with a varied reading diet supports children to experience the scope of what written language can convey and the range of ways in which it can do so.

The content of what they consume also provides examples of subject matter that is worthy of print. Through the range of text types, genres, themes and topics they encounter, children learn that texts can serve varied functions. They can be a source of entertainment to be read at our leisure and a source of information to expand our knowledge and understanding of ourselves and the world around us. Through the casts of characters they meet, readers forge connections that enhance their investment in the narratives that are spun.

These reading experiences strengthen the child's reading capabilities over time and in turn support them in building a body of reference that not only informs what they come to expect from books, but also shapes their writing. A simple example of this is the way in which children relish the opportunity to use a new word they come across in every possible piece of writing they produce, even when it is wholly inappropriate. A word like 'gargantuan', for example, would typically be a word that would pique a child's interest. It is a great word and feels good to chew in your mouth as you say it but peppering it in every other sentence or piece of writing can quickly make it lose its effect. Going through the process of this kind of saturation and evaluation is all part of the necessary learning about how to build the knowledge, competence and confidence to choose words judiciously for optimum effect. Children will also draw on the content of what they read to inform their choices about the narrative structure, subjects and themes of what they write. What and who they encounter in the books they read gives them a bank of reference to draw from. The sum of their reading experiences provides children with a sense of what they should come to expect from the literary space and becomes the well from which they draw to guide how they might emulate this in their own writing.

DEFINING AND DEVELOPING WRITER IDENTITY

If the content that children consume is so instrumental in shaping children's ideas about how writing works and informs their understanding of the literary space, what happens when the casts and content of the books that they encounter do not reflect the realities of the world in which they live? In this section we will contemplate how we support children to develop a positive writer identity and the role of representative literature in fortifying this.

Nurturing the development of children's writer identity requires us to attend to the different facets, detailed in the graphic in Figure 6.1, that work together to support a child's capacity to identify as a writer. Just as we did earlier with reading, we will reflect on each of these components to consider not only the ways in which they work together in helping to formulate a sense of writer identity, but also how these encourage a re-evaluation of what it means to have an inclusive ethos and practice.

THE KEY COMPONENTS OF WRITER IDENTITY

THE ABILITY

Communicating legible, coherent and engaging thoughts and ideas on paper involves a complex and multi-layered series of processes and actions that must work effectively and simultaneously to produce the desired outcome. To feel able requires us to have the words and an appreciation of how language works, as well as the knowledge, confidence and skill to mould it into written form to articulate what you want to say. The physical, cognitive and linguistic demands of this process can be overwhelming even at the most accomplished levels, let alone in the early stages of developing competency. To feel able, children need

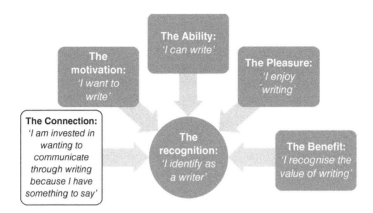

Figure 6.1   Key Components of Writer Identity ©CLPE 2023

the opportunity to write for purpose and pleasure in a range of contexts. This breadth of experiences should support them in developing an appreciation for the range of benefits this form of communication can afford. Children should not feel that their core purpose for writing is to be at the mercy of the red pen. They must grow to appreciate that we write for many reasons, such as to:

- help us make sense of our thoughts and feelings
- communicate ideas
- organise ourselves, our days and our spaces
- have a creative outlet
- entertain ourselves and others
- encourage others to think
- challenge thinking
- provide information.

They must have meaningful opportunities to engage in this breadth and range of writing experiences to broaden their appreciation of what this skill can afford them. Our teaching of writing requires us to build children's knowledge of language and how it works, teach the mechanics involved in the process while also helping them to appreciate the benefit and sustain their motivation and stamina.

In the first year of the project the children responded really well to the point that we had children writing in the playground, writing at home, writing poetry and even now, in the second year of the project, this has continued. They're much more willing to express themselves through writing channels and explore ideas more creatively and individually. There is definitely a sense that they have more ownership of what they are doing.

Senior leader

THE MOTIVATION, BENEFIT AND PLEASURE

Never before have the children loved writing so much. The enjoyment in lessons is incredible, with our most reluctant writers now engaged.

Senior leader

How do children engage with writing in your classroom? Are they always ready with pens poised, excited at the prospect of putting pen to paper, or do they reluctantly drag their pens across the page hoping that whatever they feel able to commit will suffice? You will invariably have children that sit on all points of this scale of enthusiasm. Take a moment to consider your current class. Note who, on average, sits where on the scale detailed. Create a table to record this such as the one shown in Figure 6.2.

Our children are now seeing themselves as writers. They understand the purpose of what they are writing and see how they can take ownership of it. They have engaged with the opportunities to express their creativity and individuality within their writing. The children have engaged with the range of authors and been able to identify themselves within the authors they have worked with. They have shown a real love of reading and writing throughout all the units.

Senior leader

Level of engagement	Children's names	Total number of children
Doesn't write		
Writes reluctantly		
Writes occasionally		
Writes with encouragement		
Writes without prompting		
Writes with confidence		
Writes enthusiastically		

Figure 6.2   Assessing Writer Engagement ©CLPE 2023

What do your reflections suggest about children's engagement and enthusiasm for writing? Are there a disproportionate number of children located in any one of the sections of the table? What might this indicate? If you have children located on the less enthusiastic parts of the scale, what might be causing the disinterest or reluctance? How would you typify their experiences of writing and how might these have contributed to their feelings towards it? Conversely, if you have a high proportion of children located in the latter part of the scale, what do you think fuels their enthusiasm and engagement?

Generally, our children are more confident. They're more confident and they feel much more represented. We're seeing children be more creative and being more open and being more free in how they represent themselves in their own writing. Whereas before my children definitely felt like they had to fit in, fit your box, fit a kind of norm of what stories look like. Whereas now they're much more free and open to just what they feel is them.

Class teacher

To help us further contemplate the way writing might be perceived in your classroom take a moment to consider the different types of writing your children engaged in over the course of the last week.

TAKE TIME TO CONSIDER

What were the different forms of writing your children had the opportunity to produce last week?

Review the list you have produced and consider what the function was of each type of writing. Create a table (such as the example show in Figure 6.3) to support your thinking.

How varied were the purposes for writing? Did children focus on one type of writing more than another? Is this a fair representation of an average week? What might the types of writing convey to the children about the function of writing? This last question is important in supporting our considerations about how our practice and provision communicate the purpose and value of writing to our learners. These experiences will shape children's appreciation of the multi-purpose nature of writing as well as their motivation to engage with it. Developing this appreciation and supporting their growth as writers will also involve explicitly exploring the role of reading in shaping their writing. Thinking about all of the children in our class and all of the writing experiences and opportunities available to them helps us to identify and think about children who may not be seeing themselves as writers. This can help us to consider the possible correlation between how provision can impact a child's self-perception.

Function	Leisure and pleasure	Note thoughts or ideas	Communicate thoughts or ideas	Functional	Creative	Present learning
Examples	Journalling	Text marking, writing drafts, notes	Mind maps, presentations, posters, flyers	To do lists, shopping lists, instructions, labels	Stories, poetry	Formal writing tasks
No. of opportunities for your children to engage in this type of writing						

Figure 6.3   Reflecting on Range of Writing Opportunities ©CLPE 2023

When children are afforded the opportunity to do free writing a lot of them are leaning on their own experiences and drawing upon them. The project has given the teachers confidence to allow them that freedom. It also helps that the children are not nervous to share something that might be different to their peers.

Senior leader

THE CONNECTION

Deep, authentic connection involves the desire to communicate, the belief that what you want to say is of value or interest and the freedom to draw on your lived experiences without feeling a sense of inadequacy. It can be quite revelatory for children to learn that for many authors the seeds of stories often start with observations of everyday occurrences. This insight can support them in appreciating their scope to build story worlds starting from a familiar base. While the familiarity can provide children with the confidence to move forward in shaping fictional worlds, this will only be effective if the children feel confident enough to share personal points of reference – be they cultural, routine, or otherwise. If children inter- nalise a sense that aspects of their lives or identity are not worthy of the page, then such self-censorship can inhibit their creative output.

The training with Joseph Coelho made it feel okay to encourage children to draw on their own prior knowledge and made us appreciate how important it is to validate that. As teachers, we are often really guilty of trying to get kids to come up with the most amaz- ing, elaborate stories. And for him to say, it's okay if they want to base their story in Lidl because that's a valid point of reference helped to shift our thinking. What was also made clear is that it's our job to then pull out other creative elements, such as asking what could happen in Lidl and what might the carrot do? Through this questioning the story can then build from there. When we started to do that and allow children to base their stories in familiar places like the local Lidl store or on the bus or in their tower block and not force them to be on a planet in space or a similar abstract context that they didn't have an experience of they then felt safer to take risks and we could then help them to get going with the story. I feel like that was really empowering for us to come away with that message to then tell other staff and then see the children being able to not be as fearful about being creative.

Class teacher

Two key anecdotes shared by Verna Wilkins and Darren Chetty 30 years apart powerfully convey the potential detrimental impact on reader, writer and learner identity when this freedom is compromised.

Tamarind Books was founded by Verna Wilkins in 1987 following a worrying interaction with her then five-year-old son. She recounted in her Patrick Hardy lecture titled, 'The Right to be Seen', in 2008 that he had come home from school with a self-made book titled 'This is Me'. Wilkins had noticed that her son had chosen to colour himself in using a pink crayon and when she offered him a brown crayon to use instead, he declined the offer and explained that he had to use the pink crayon because it was for a book. As Wilkins has recounted many times since this incident, her son, a young boy of Grenadian heritage, had at the age of five internalised the idea that someone who looked like him did not belong in the pages of books. This prompted her to research what might be at the root of this assumption. It was evident from her investigations that children from racially minoritised backgrounds were significantly under-represented in the literature available to them, which could reasonably lead to young readers drawing the same conclusion as her son. Driven by her concerns about the damaging implications, Wilkins was inspired to remedy this by publishing books that would counteract this erasure by centring Black protagonists and featuring multi-cultural casts of characters.

In his essay contribution for the *Good Immigrant* (2016), published almost 30 years later, Darren Chetty reflected on how challenging the children in his multi-cultural class of children in the borough of Newham, East London, found it to incorporate protagonists of colour in their stories despite being encouraged to draw on the people in their own life and community for inspiration. When a child did attempt to do this and was chosen to share their work with the rest of the class, they were quickly corrected by a peer who expressed, *'You can't say that! Stories have to be about white people.'* This feedback conveyed an underlying belief that books and the literary space were understood to be the exclusive domain of white characters.

Both experiences would suggest that, despite concerted efforts by advocates, activists, librarians, independent publishers, independent booksellers, parents and educators, the UK children's publishing landscape has lacked sufficient diversity of representation in its casts of characters for a long time resulting in limited availability of quality representative titles on classroom bookshelves.

The three-decade time gap between these two accounts not only highlights how slow progress has been in this area, but also illustrates the consequences of disproportionately under-representative texts on both children's reading diets and writing choices. The absence of characters of colour in the books children encountered in both instances had set a ceiling on expectations in this regard. Both accounts serve as examples of the way such erasure can be internalised and perpetuated, which raises concerns about the wider ramifications of such erasure on learner self-perception and agency.

Five more years on from Darren Chetty's experience, the contributions of children and reflections of teachers participating in our Reflecting Realities in the Classroom project further corroborate the insights shared by Chetty and Wilkins. In this project we supported the teachers to review their book stock, to build reader identity and an inclusive reading culture and to engage with authors of colour to understand their books, their processes and their motivations. In both years of the project to date we have collected a range of evidence in which teachers have observed the children in their school sharing insights into their home life and culture in a way that they hadn't done before.

Teachers reported that children were making links between the characters they encountered in the representative titles and aspects of their own lives. They observed similarities in hairstyles, skin tone and family dynamics which inspired the confidence to draw on this for their own writing. Working alongside authors of colour also provided the children with the opportunity to not only be inspired, but also appreciate and apply authentic creative approaches to their own writing process. This created a positive shift in attitude, engagement and output, making for a more vibrant, creative, uplifting community of writers and learning culture.

> *Through my observations, I notice that the children seem more confident and able now to make up their own stories and incorporate parts of their own personality. The impact of this spans beyond the children directly involved in the project. One girl in Year 5, for example, incorporated details about the curl pattern in her hair in her writing. For many of the children across year groups we're seeing children draw on their own experiences to inform and shape their writing. And I think that has got to be coming through the fact that they're reading stories that have these details and representations within them.*

Class teacher

If marginalised children don't feel able to write people who look like them or who share social, cultural or ethnic commonalities into their own works of fiction this raises a number of questions for us as teachers such as: what other ways are children self-censoring, what other aspects of themselves are they holding back, how does this inform their learner identity, how might it hinder their reader and writer identity and how does this impact on their relationship with the learning space?

By reflecting on these questions we are ultimately considering what is involved in affirming a young learner's identity in a way that ensures that they have licence to fully be and express themselves in the learning space. Wilkins' young son and Chetty's class of Key Stage 1 children had learnt very early on in their schooling to self-censor in line with the literary content they had consumed. It is difficult to determine how far such self-censorship might extend and how this might compromise the learning experience for marginalised learners. One way we might be able to counteract this is to consider how we provide each child with the licence to be their authentic selves through affirming practices that support them to feel valued and comfortable enough to bring much more of themselves across the classroom threshold to engage in their learning without feeling inhibited. As explored in Chapter 2, and as we will go on to discuss in the final chapter, while books are an integral piece of the puzzle when considering inclusivity, we must consider all aspects of practice to ensure a meaningful inclusive teaching provision and learning culture.

CHAPTER 7

DEVELOPING AUTHENTIC CREATIVE WRITING PRACTICES IN THE CLASSROOM

> I'm a writer so I am always thinking in terms of books and literature and so reflecting realities means for me, do the books on your shelf, in your home, the books you use in your classroom, the books in your library, do the books you hand out to kids, whether your students of [sic] children, reflect the kind of world that we live in – because if they don't then that's where things should start.
>
> There is always a call to diversify the kinds of books we publish and promote, but more important than that is we need to diversify our lives, that should be the first step to create an equitable world for our children – we have to make sure our lives reflect the kind of world we want for them.
>
> Kwame Alexander

Kwame Alexander is an American poet, educator, producer and number one *New York Times* bestselling author of 39 books, including *Why Fathers Cry at Night* (2023), *An American Story* (2023), *The Door of No Return* (2023), *Becoming Muhammad Ali* (co-authored with James Patterson, 2020), *Booked* (2016), which was highly commended for the 2017 CLiPPA, *Rebound* (2018), which was shortlisted for the UK Carnegie Medal and the CLiPPA in 2019, and *The Undefeated* (2020), the National Book Award nominee, Newbery Honor and Caldecott Medal-winning picturebook illustrated by Kadir Nelson. He is the executive producer, showrunner and writer of *The Crossover* TV series, based on his Newbery-Medal-winning novel of the same name, which premiered on Disney+ in April 2023.

The quote above is from Kwame's blog *Reflecting Realities*, written for CLPE in 2020.

Find out more:

In the previous chapter we looked at the connections between reading and writing and the importance of supporting children to develop a 'writer identity' as they become competent and confident readers and writers. We looked at the kinds of classroom practice that supports all children, and particularly those whose backgrounds and cultures are not traditionally reflected in children's literature, to develop their identity in an authentic and supportive way.

This chapter is about the writing process – the process that an author who is creating something that someone else will read will go through. We think about the importance of not just seeing yourself on the page but also seeing creators who are like you, or who share similar backgrounds and how that makes a difference to writing outcomes. We also think about the practices and the structures that need to be in place for all children to develop as writers who are able to create confidently, authentically and creatively.

THE COMPLEXITY AND DEMANDS OF THE WRITING PROCESS

The distance a child must travel from having a thought to articulating it on paper is a long and winding one. They must first formulate a thought or idea in their mind that they wish to communicate. They must internally articulate it to themselves and then consider how best to express it in a way that would make sense to someone else. They then need to determine how best to phrase it for the purposes of the page because written language is distinctive from spoken language. They will have to consider which words most effectively convey their thoughts. They will have to pool their knowledge of grammar to determine how to organise and punctuate the words on the page. In reading back what they have written, they must consider whether the text fulfils their intention and if adjustments need to be made to achieve their ideal outcome and enhance the impact. These steps of mental, oral and written drafting, editing and refinement are not necessarily as linear a process as outlined and will often involve a back and forth dance between the various stages in this process. Children undertake this sophisticated process while learning about the world around them and still developing their communication skills, building their vocabulary bank, evolving their understanding of how language works, acquiring their knowledge of how written language works and acquiring the skills of putting all of this into practice for optimal effect. Parallel to this, they are also dealing with the personal, social, emotional and mental load of navigating school life.

As teachers of writing, it is crucial that our recognition of the inherent complexity and demands of the writing process inform our considerations about how best to facilitate this process. Holding all the parts of this process in our heads, applying them all in the right way at the right time while maintaining the necessary stamina to continually commit ourselves during our formative stage of development can be tremendously challenging. It is therefore totally understandable that as teachers we will seek to compartmentalise and simplify the different elements of this process. And while this is appropriate to some extent, leaning too rigidly into formulaic approaches or prescriptive steps to facilitate writing can compromise the process and result in stifled output.

Writing is a creative undertaking that requires creative licence. It can be messy and full of stops and starts that take the writer in a range of directions before they come to an end point with which they are satisfied. Writing can take many forms and be for a range of purposes and audiences, from deeply personal writing that is for your eyes only, to writing that seeks to galvanise the masses. The breadth and chaos of this creative endeavour can therefore be quite challenging to locate within the neat confines of a one-hour literacy lesson in which you hope to be able to teach some content along with a series of skills that should result in at least a page of writing in every child's exercise books by the time the bell chimes for break. Spending time contemplating this tension and considering how to alleviate it provides a real opportunity to unlock every child's deep writing potential. We spend a great deal of time planning and preparing lessons that will build children's knowledge, understanding and skill of the different components of writing. In order to support them in channelling and honing their own unique writing voice, it is also useful to consider how we might draw from accomplished writers and their approaches to writing to bolster our work in this area.

Every writer will have their preferred way of working and will draw on a range of methods and practices that support their process. Some have a clear vision of what they want to write from the outset, while for others the focus evolves over time; some like the solitude of writing in the early hours before the world is awake, others thrive from the support and feedback of a writing group; some will research extensively before putting pen to paper, others will investigate as they go; some will doodle, others will sketch; some will collage, others will write in journals; while others will type straight onto their laptop. By working alongside creatives as part of our professional development programme to support teachers with their thinking in this area, we have had the privilege of learning first-hand just how varied the process is from artist to artist.

WRITING ROLE MODELS

Through our Reflecting Realities in the Classroom project we were keen to extend and consolidate the learning from our previous programmes by determining how working alongside creatives of colour might impact on children's writing process. As discussed in the previous chapter the value of role models in the learning space is key to inspiring young learners. It is important that children encounter adults from all backgrounds, engaging across all spheres of society, in a range of disciplines. Such role models are crucial to challenging prejudices and key to inspiring aspiration.

Participating teachers were open and honest about how their understanding around the importance of representative and inclusive literature had shifted since engaging with the project and how limited their knowledge was of children's authors and illustrators of colour before engaging in the project.

> *Although we have made efforts in the past, our children definitely haven't felt represented or able to talk confidently about themselves as writers and identify themselves in literature. Since participating in the project, we now hear the children talk enthusiastically about the fact that they see themselves in books. They've had the opportunity to see and hear from authors of colour that they never knew existed and that's been really mind*

opening. It's been really powerful for them to see the faces of the actual people behind the books and realise who they were and actually that, that could be them.

There was a perception that most authors had to be old and that definitely came through when we did quizzes with the children inviting them to think about who they identify authors to be. Most of the time the children chose older white males.

Senior leader

Teachers have shared that investing in more representative stock and ensuring increased visibility of book creators of colour has broadened children's understanding of who can do this type of work. The work the children have engaged with as part of the project has supported children to 'realise that they can become writers' and that 'they can become an amazing poet or short story writer'. The children 'see themselves as writers' and know that 'anyone can be an author and anyone can be an illustrator'. These are important shifts particularly when considered within the context of Verna Wilkins' and Darren Chetty's anecdotes shared in the last chapter. What was particularly striking was that a number of the authors participating in the project shared how their own early experiences of under-representation had impacted their creative choices in similar ways to those described by Wilkins and Chetty. It was both humbling and tremendously moving to have them be so open in sharing such personal insights and see how the participating teachers were fuelled by this to work with their children to end this cycle. Working alongside these authors developing an appreciation for what and who inspires their work and learning about their creative process provided the children with fantastically inspiring role models and content to empower them to own and evolve their writer identities.

The participating teachers reported that because of the project they had increased the profile of authors, illustrators and poets by taking the time to talk about them and their works. Some chose to share images of these book creators as part of this process in lessons and through displays. This ensured that children had an increased awareness and familiarity of book creators, particularly authors, illustrators and poets of colour. One teacher reflected that:

this programme has massively, massively impacted the children's knowledge of texts and authorship definitely. I've noticed my children saying things like, 'Oh, that looks in a similar style to Ken Wilson-Max.' Or, 'Oh, I think this might be an Adeola book because it looks like this.' Or, 'Oh, that sounds a little bit like Valerie Bloom's poem.'

This not only supports aspiration and challenges prejudice, but it also creates the groundwork for developing children's appreciation of differences in aesthetic, written and illustrative styles and encourages them to make intertextual links. It develops their appreciation of the art and craft of writing at a much deeper level.

As part of the programme, we produced a series of videos of authors of colour discussing their process and sharing their work. The children had the opportunity to follow sequences of work inspired by a title from each author which supported them through the creative process towards publishing their own writing. These publications included their own picturebooks, short story collections and whole-class poetry anthologies. Participating teachers observed notable shifts in the ways in which children were engaging in the learning space. Children drew connections with the content of the books they studied and seemed to be more open in sharing aspects of themselves and their home life in ways that they hadn't done before. One teacher commented that, *'At various points children have excitedly expressed, "that's me," and have been asking for more new books like this, while parents have taken the time to thank me for promoting and using more varied texts.'* Encountering characters from similar backgrounds and seeing the authors talk about their own experiences created the opportunity and way in for children to draw connections and incorporate these elements into their own work. There was a sense of pride, a stronger sense of agency and an elevated meaningfulness in the work they were producing. One teacher reflected that one child:

> *showed lots of engagement throughout the series of lessons and enjoyed the addition of picturebooks where they felt more represented in our book corner. They began reading books they hadn't experienced before and sharing these with the class. These books also gave them more confidence when talking about their own family experiences.*

> *Working alongside creatives has improved our students' engagement as they love seeing them in the videos and feel a personal connection to them. Working with creatives has vastly improved our knowledge and understanding of an authentic writing process – hearing the way they gather ideas, plan their pieces, how they work in rough and then refine has been so valuable.*

Senior leader

A number of teachers also reflected that through the openness and sharing that the work invited they felt that they were able to foster stronger relationships with their children. These testimonies highlight the power of affirming practices referred to in an earlier chapter. Children felt comfortable enough to commit themselves fully and openly to the creative process, allowing them to challenge themselves to produce high-quality work that was meaningful to them. This creative, tailored and considered approach to literacy is what defines the core essence of CLPE'S approach to teaching. This is ultimately what teaching seeks to achieve, getting the best out of the learner to help them be all that they can be.

EMULATING AUTHENTIC WRITING PRACTICES

This extensive body of work has allowed us to appreciate the value of demystifying the writing process and inspiring budding writers by creating an environment in which authentic writing practices can be emulated. In every subject area and discipline, we look to the experts to guide our learning, it therefore makes sense to draw on the knowledge and experience of this body of professional creatives to inform our approaches to the teaching of writing in the classroom. By learning about the different ways that writers approach writing children not only learn to appreciate such variation, but also are given permission to attempt varied ways into writing themselves. It encourages them to act like writers and to be led by considerations about what it is they want to say, how they want to say it, how it might be received and determine what choices they will need to make to achieve this. This in turn will result in more considered, creative and varied content across the class.

Although creatives each have their own unique approach to writing, through our work with author illustrators in particular as part of our Power of Pictures programme we have been able to identify the core common threads across the approaches that creatives take and distil these into the graphic summarised in Figure 7.1. Every creative will go through the process of generating and exploring ideas for their writing, considering what they want to say, what and who they want to write about and what they want to explore through their writing. This ideation phase can be informed by people watching, capturing conversational snippets in a journal or sketching moments of life as they pass us by. They might be inspired by reading and researching into a particular topic, public figure or historical era. In other instances, an object might be the starting point or an aspect of popular culture or societal challenge. The thoughts and ideas of this initial phase might be captured in sketch books, writing journals, voice notes, mapped out on boards or laid out on tables. Through this phase the writer formulates ideas about the direction that they might take.

Our children are enthused and have greater writing stamina. Through this process they have developed and increased their autonomy within the ideation process, which has been brilliant. *They have taken responsibility and enhanced their school work with research at home (e.g. one child who was developing a narrative about moving to Asia learnt Japanese using Duolingo to insert dialogue into their story). The way the English lessons have become just the spark/ignition for their learning/ideas is remarkable and an amazing testament to both the CLPE units and the class teacher's delivery.*

Senior leader

In the creation phase, they will develop their cast, the narrative, themes and content. The choices they make will not necessarily be definitive or static. Their characters, casts and storylines are likely to undergo many iterations during the creation phase. Seemingly insignificant details at the outset might blossom over the course of writing into becoming an integral part of the story. Conversely there may be large parts of a story that are abandoned by a change in direction. There is a necessary permission that must be given to exploration, play and experimentation during this phase. Allowing space for drafting that enables a process of refinement is a crucial part of the process.

The act of reflection threads throughout the creative process and ensuring dedicated opportunities for this is key. The capacity to evaluate whether the writing is fulfilling the author's intention and effectively satisfying its purpose requires a commitment to drafting and redrafting. To undergo this process authors must have resilience, stamina, objectivity, critical reflection and the capacity to be able to drop large chunks of their writing. Through creative writing we can nurture these crucial skills and attributes in our children. Many authors will have an ongoing dialogue with an editor to support them to reflect on their work and refine the choices they have made until they feel satisfied that the work is ready for publication. Replicating this dynamic by using response partners as part of peer-to-peer support can transform the writing practices and culture of the classroom.

THE CYCLE OF CREATIVITY

Figure 7.1   Authentic Writing Process ©CLPE 2020

The opportunity to work up writing to a published outcome is an important part of making the process purposeful. Having a desired end point in mind is crucial to helping children to hone their work and to be more considered about their intended audience and the impact they want the piece to have. The choices will differ depending on what form the publication will take. It might take the form of performance including examples such as a speech, poetry reading, play or presentation. Each of these types of live action publication will require distinctive considerations to ensure that the intention of the writing is effectively communicated and that it achieves the desired effect. Similarly, the choices we make about content that we are developing for written publications which might come in the form of a poster, set of instructions, booklet or short story will also vary. Through such considerations we will need to undertake an ongoing process of refinement to the writing to ensure that we are satisfied that it will deliver in fulfilling its purpose. Working towards a published piece also aids them in building stamina and resilience. Learning from experiences of professional creatives we gain important insights into what is involved in working a piece of writing up to final publication. We learn about the decisions that lead to determining what makes the final cut and why some things are designated to the cutting room floor. This supports us to appreciate that it's okay to let go of content and keep our focus on what we want to say and how best to say it.

    This cycle of creativity can be emulated in the classroom by creating opportunities for children to adopt such practices as part of their writing process. This would involve allowing space for the children to meaningfully engage in the different stages and providing the tools and means to be able to do this. For example, as a very basic requirement, all children should have their own writing journals. These are distinctively different to their everyday exercise books. Their writing journals are a place to capture thoughts and ideas in any form they choose to. This might be the place in which they sketch ideas for different characters to serve as a casting exercise for prospective stories. They might note words they like the sound of. They might note ideas for storylines or create collages of images that inspire them. The journals should not be subject to marking but instead should serve as a bank of reference and inspiration for the child.

We introduced this as a requirement at the start of our Reflecting Realities in the Classroom research project and encouraged the teachers to ensure that they gifted every child in their Year 3 class with their own journal. A number of the participating teachers commented on how this had encouraged and supported children's volitional writing, inspiring them to want to write more in their free time. We encountered instances such as children choosing to write short stories at home to children asking for paper so that they could draw and write during their playtimes. This enthusiasm was in part sparked by giving children the licence, choice and space to write what they wanted to write. The journals are a perfect means of emulating the messiness of authentic writing processes. They give children a place to explore and try things out without the weight of worrying about how the teacher might judge it. This helps to encourage the experimentation and risk-taking that are important parts of developing ideas for writing. It also enables them to experience the more personal purposes and benefits of writing.

By working alongside creatives through this research project, teachers were able to hear first-hand the crucial role that writing groups and editors played in helping them to develop their work. We encourage children to re-read their work to check it makes sense and often enlist their peers as editing partners. But learning more about the value of peer critique and ongoing dialogue gave us the opportunity to consider how this might translate in the classroom. We encouraged teachers to think about how they might organise this in the classroom. In some instances, this would work well by grouping children into pairs, in others it might be more effective to group children into groups of three. They should have opportunities to pause at various stages to reflect on different aspects. They might want to articulate their ideas to help hone the direction they might want to take. They could share a segment of their writing to reflect on whether it's conveying the right amount of emotion or effectively communicating the core message. They might be unsure about how best to tie up their piece. Having the opportunity to engage in this kind of dialogue with a response partner gives them the time to trial and develop ideas, exploring the direction they might take with a storyline or developing their cast. Given how demanding it is to commit our thoughts and ideas to paper it can be challenging to receive and respond to feedback. If having an open dialogue with response partners is not a standard practice in your classroom it will be important to model this. Children will need to be supported to develop the skills to be effective response partners, who are able to read, listen and respond to their peer's work in progress with sensitivity and thoughtfulness. They must be given the language and skills to be able to offer constructive and considered feedback. As recipients of such feedback, children must also be guided on how to receive and act on suggestions.

Time must be designated to enable children to develop and refine their work with a view to publishing it in some form. A published outcome helps us to elevate the child's consciousness of audience, which in turn helps to hone their creative choices. Hearing first-hand picturebook author/illustrators Ken Wilson-Max and Lucy Farfort discussing the thinking behind some of their creative choices in their published titles helped to inform children's own considerations when producing their own picturebooks. One teacher observed that one child in their class was:

> *highly imaginative and very engaged in creating ideas and developing characters and story. They thought very carefully about word choice and structure of the story and how the information was to be laid out across each double page spread. It was entertaining to read.*

It was refreshing to hear colleagues talk about how they delighted in reading their children's work and witnessing their humour, creativity and individuality come through. This is very different to the monotony that can come from marking 30 sets of almost identical pieces of writing that are in keeping with the learning objective but lack the innovation and individuality that was evident through the work of the children participating in this project. Not only did this shift the teacher's experiences; it also shifted the way children interacted with their learning, with one child commenting that he enjoyed the designing aspect of the process, particularly the front-papers and endpapers, explaining, *'it meant that I could be free with my choice and draw a rainbow, which is something I rarely see'.* He went on to explain in more detail, that he enjoys having a choice in his learning because he can bring in his own ideas, which are wide and varied. In another class, the teacher shared that one child commented that:

> *I really enjoyed the drawing and colouring of the picturebook because it made me feel very relaxed. I enjoyed creating my story board, especially the writing and where it should go on the page. I was able to use my own ideas rather than just writing on lines in a book. I found creating an idea for my picturebook tricky. I had so many so it was hard to choose.*

This sense of ease, creative dilemma and enthusiasm expressed is quite a contrast to the way some children talk about how they feel about their literacy lessons.

The final picturebooks that were produced embodied a rich range of themes, storylines and interesting protagonists. It was evident that children were invested in the stories they had crafted from the carefully considered end papers, to the thoughtful dedication in one instance to the source of inspiration, author Ken Wilson-Max, to the fact that one of the children even dressed as the character they created for World Book Day. One participating school took this one step further and arranged it so that their children's picturebooks could be displayed alongside Ken Wilson-Max's titles in their local independent bookshop. The affirming power of Year 3 children seeing their books in a bookshop alongside other books is immense. It will have formed an important core memory that recognises the value of their creative output and conveys to them the scope of possibility.

The practices and approaches necessary to embed this cycle of creativity helps to shift the learning culture towards one in which children have a sense of creative autonomy; they engage with their peers not as fellow learners but more as fellow writers. The classroom becomes a community of writers engrossed in developing ideas, engaged in rich conversations about their work in progress, invested in the output and feeling a sense of accomplishment with the unique publications. This kind of culture and community leads to a richer, elevated, deeper and more meaningful learning experience for all.

CHAPTER 8

REFLECTING REALITIES: INFORMING, SHAPING AND SHIFTING SCHOOL CULTURE

> The Romantic poets gave us the idea that writing is about inspiration. No bad thing. It's lovely when we are inspired by something we see or hear or imagine. But there are other kinds of writing that start from exploring, asking questions, recording what other people say, looking at old photos and documents. I've found that a good shape or pattern for these kinds of thoughts are poems but others might find other forms.
>
> Finally, fascinating moments come when we share these stories and start to get a sense of who we are in the world, different but similar, living lives with a mix of fun, tragedy, hope, despair and much more besides.
>
> Michael Rosen

Michael Rosen is one of Britain's best-loved writers and performance poets for children and adults. He was the Children's Laureate from 2007–9 and has published over 200 books for children and adults, including his non-fiction book *The Missing* (2021) and *A Great Big Cuddle* (2017), which won the CLiPPA in 2016, and the CLiPPA 2021 winning *On The Move*. He is currently Professor of Children's Literature at Goldsmiths, University of London, where he co-devised and teaches critical approaches to reading on an MA in Children's Literature, having done the same at Birkbeck, University of London. He has taught on MA courses in universities since 1994. Michael is a patron of CLPE.

The quote here is from Michael's blog about *The Missing*, written for CLPE in 2020.

Find out more:

This book has been shaped by what we have learnt from our Reflecting Realities body of research, from the *Reflecting Realities Survey of Ethnic Representation in Children's Literature* (2021, 2022) and from our Reflecting Realities in the Classroom research project. The case for the value of ethnically inclusive and representative literature is generally accepted as an ethical imperative. Through the two key strands of this work we have aimed to extend the ethical argument by developing thinking about the impact of meaningful representation. The Reflecting Realities annual surveys have provided a rich data set that have helped us to better understand the quantity and quality of ethnically representative literature currently available in the UK children's market. Through the review process we have been able to determine the features that define high-quality representative literature and distinguish this from the common components of books that fall short of this standard. As in the annual surveys, we have attempted to distil this learning and offer guidance in this book that not only serves publishers to do better but also supports educators who are key consumers to be more discerning. The impact of these surveys has contributed to raising consciousness within the industry and supported the acceleration of the increased production of representative literature.

The Reflecting Realities in the Classroom research project sought to determine what it meant to reflect children's realities in the classroom and consider how this might impact learners and learning. Schools generally don't need to be convinced of the value of inclusive representative literature. However, the way this is interpreted and put into practice will vary from setting to setting. As a basic minimum schools will seek to add representative titles to their book corners or school libraries, if they are lucky enough to have one. This investment can be in the form of a random selection of titles or a methodical review of stock currently available followed by a comprehensive restock. In some instances, these titles will form the basis of a special display or a demarcated 'diversity' shelf and in others these will become an integrated part of the book corner.

Through our Reflecting Realities in the Classroom project, we have learnt that, whatever the level of investment and however we choose to arrange these titles, such considerations are really only the tip of a very deep iceberg, as summarised in the graphic in Figure 8.1. By assessing the extent to which our book stock is inclusive and representative and evaluating the impact of such literature on children's learner identities and our learning culture it encourages deeper considerations about the extent to which all aspects of our provision are inclusive. Through such questioning and honest assessment, what begins to unfold is the extent to which our core provision is or is not inclusive. So what begins initially as an evaluation of our book stock can result in a systematic drilling down through the iceberg to get to the fundamental question of whether or not we are meeting the needs and interests of all of our learners and therefore whether or not our provision is truly inclusive.

In terms of our library stock I think it would be fair to say that we had representative book stock. The same could be said for our book corners but despite this it may not have been obvious, they were there, but they weren't obvious, if that makes sense. So, we had the book stock, but we just didn't know how to promote them, how to use them, and they weren't embedded in our curriculum at all.

Class teacher

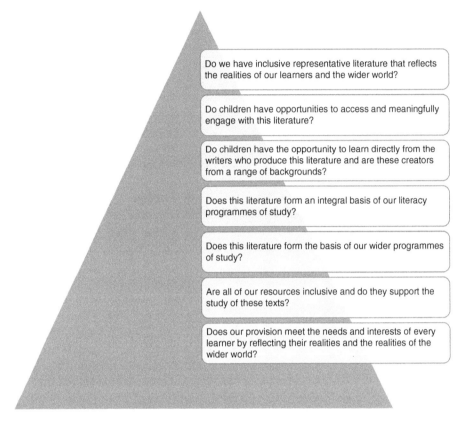

Figure 8.1   Assessing all Layers of Provision to Ensure Meaningful Inclusive Practice ©CLPE 2023

We had always viewed our *Reflecting Realities* annual survey as the first step of a longer process towards ensuring better more inclusive practices in schools. The increase in the volume of representative literature has resulted in increased choice which invites deeper considerations about the opportunities this affords within the classroom.

The discourse around the need for more inclusive books has coincided with conversations about the lack of opportunity and investment in writers of colour. The implications of this in the classroom are twofold in terms of how we teach who writers are and what writers do. First, a key part of our role as teachers involves equipping enabling and empowering children to be and do the best that they can. We aim to build a foundation of knowledge, skills, curiosity, confidence and resilience that will sustain them long after they have left the primary phase of their schooling. In terms of the teaching of writing they must have the opportunity to encounter writers from a range of backgrounds to help challenge any mis-conceptions about what and who a writer is and can be. And if such misconceptions or prejudices haven't begun to form roots, then the exposure to writers of colour will be crucial to diminishing the possibility of any ceilings forming that may inhibit the creative aspirations of young learners. Second, writing is often taught as a functional enterprise that forms a slot in our daily timetable which limits the opportunity for children to appreciate the breadth of purpose and power of writing. By ensuring that our children have the opportunity to engage with professional writers to understand the authentic creative processes involved in producing the books in their book corner, they develop an appreciation for the sophistication of this craft. We tend to teach them to adopt the behaviours and approaches of scientists, historians and artists etc. when teaching the different areas of study but do we teach them to think and behave like writers? Do we encourage them to revere writing as a professional discipline and not just something we have to do after break time? Writers across disciplines shape thinking, culture and society. This is an important responsibility and a powerful enterprise. Developing a learning culture that platforms positive writing role models from a range of backgrounds and emulates authentic creative processes shifts the dynamic from a classroom of learners to an autonomous writing community of creatives working together to produce original, varied and interesting content.

Re-evaluating our book stock and the producers of these titles is only worthwhile if we then ask whether we are creating opportunities for meaningful engagement with these texts. If they're only ever brought out for special occasions or specific topic work, then we in effect end up mirroring the lack of representative, inclusive content and its marginalisation across the arts and all spheres of society. Undertaking a text-mapping exercise to determine the extent to which such texts form an integral basis of our literacy programmes of study supports us to ascertain the status afforded these titles. Ensuring that they form part of our mainstream provision endorses their literary merit, elevates their value and goes some way towards counteracting the aforementioned marginalisation.

The increased consciousness regarding our literacy provision that the representative stock triggers also invites reflections about our wider curriculum programmes of study. As we have seen through our work with schools participating in the Reflecting Realities in the Classroom project, the book stock audits, literacy curriculum reviews and professional dialogue encouraged reflections on the extent of inclusivity and balance in the history, geography and art programmes of study. This work supports us to raise questions about who and what we study and what impressions of the world this gives young learners.

The shift in practice that considerations around inclusive representative literature creates guides us towards a more tailored child-centred approach. This in turn influences the learning culture and the way in which children interact with it. By being responsive through affirming and inclusive practices we have the scope to unlock a deeper potential. This deceptively simple process of affirming children as readers and writers through meaningful engagement with authors and their works can reap profound benefits.

We have seen first-hand the tremendous impact that such access to representative literature and dedicated time to unpicking and exploring authentic creative processes can have on children's autonomy and growth as learners.

They're just so much more free, so much more responsive to creativity. They're taking more ownership of it. They're, using their wider experiences when they're writing and they realise that they don't have to fit to a set structure. We have children out in the playground, writing poetry showing their poetry and sharing poetry. They're drawing on real-life experience all the time and actually taking ownership.

Class teacher

As part of this, ensuring access to a diverse range of creators of literature is a key contributing factor. This is because diversity in authorship results in a variety of output. Each of us is an embodiment of the experiences that make up the sum of our lives. These experiences inform and shape how we view and navigate the world. They shape the stories of us, the stories we tell ourselves and the stories we craft to make sense of the world around us. My stories will be distinct from your stories and yours will be distinct compared to the next person. If the only people writing draw from a similar bank of stories this results in us only experiencing a narrow set of narratives as Chimamanda Ngozi Adichie stated in her now famous TED Talk of 2009. If you aren't part of the story worlds being portrayed the importance of your experience is diminished; it suggests that your experience isn't interesting or important enough to be included and it also suggests that your own experience must be viewed through someone else's lens – even if that lens results in reductive, stereotypical or damaging portrayals.

It is therefore important that children see themselves reflected in the book world. And see themselves and their backgrounds reflected authentically and accurately in that book world. For this we need to ensure that the books on the shelves reflect the world in which we live. We need to make sure that these books are created by authors with a range of backgrounds and viewpoints. And we need to give all the children in our classrooms the opportunity to see that people of all backgrounds, from all walks of life create the artefacts that sit on our shelves.

I think our classroom has become a space where children can see themselves, where their realities are reflected, that has given them the confidence, that's given them licence for that to be okay and for that to be part of the narrative in our school.

Class teacher

As with all aspects of our work at CLPE, the end goal has always been about supporting teachers to make classrooms the best environment they can be to enable children to have the best possible learning journey. The insights from our Reflecting Realities work have helped to consolidate our wider knowledge base about the key ingredients that support this aim. The consistent thread that runs throughout this learning is the power of authenticity and autonomy. We know that making the primary focus of all teaching about supporting children to cultivate a strong learner identity causes a crucial shift in our practice. This simple shift encourages us to centre the children and, rather than starting with the question 'what am I going to teach?', we begin by asking 'who am I going to teach?' Which leads to further questions of what their starting point is. What skills and knowledge are they bringing into the space? What are their interests and needs? How will the learning experience build on their knowledge and understanding and nurture their growth? How will it channel their curiosity and build their resilience? How will it encourage their sense of autonomy as a learner? We have found that having this principle of authentic autonomy form the foundation of our motivation and approach can significantly transform our practice and learning culture for the better, particularly when combined with the elements summarised in Figure 8.2.

KEY COMPONENTS TO ENABLE AUTONOMOUS LEARNER IDENTITY

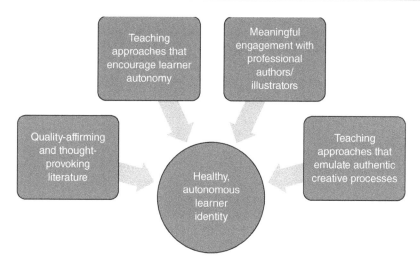

Figure 8.2   Blueprint for Autonomous Learner Identity in Literacy ©CLPE 2023

QUALITY-AFFIRMING AND THOUGHT-PROVOKING LITERATURE

Throughout this book and over the course of doing this work, the case for the benefit of quality literature as an integral part of the learning journey has been made clear. Books serve the multi-purpose role of supporting children to be literate, critical thinkers and find their feet in the learning space as a precursor to establishing their place in the world. Books have the power to bolster them, giving them the confidence and resilience required to navigate life beyond the classroom walls. As well as being a key contributing element to supporting healthy, autonomous learner identity, they provide the important base material to support learning.

TEACHING APPROACHES THAT ENCOURAGE LEARNER AUTONOMY

The knowledge base we have developed over time has taught us that creative teaching approaches give children the capacity, confidence and agency to engage in deep and meaningful learning experiences. The use of art and drama to elicit and express response, develop thinking, formulate understanding and articulate knowledge are instrumental in supporting children to access, enjoy and take control of their learning. Art is a powerful means of conveying understanding and interpreting meanings. Drama provides the means to step into the worlds of stories to build deeper connections and appreciations for the motivations, perspectives and dilemmas of characters. Learning generated from teaching approaches using these creative disciplines can take the children in lots of different directions, encouraging the teacher to go off script and be responsive to the interests and insights generated. These approaches give children the tools to take charge of their learning. By providing the space and opportunity and ensuring a mutual trust we create an environment that allows children to flourish.

> *Children have a really strong sense of identity and pride in their backgrounds. Speaking to some of the children now in the second year of the project it's clear that they have such a love for reading and such a love for books. Creativity is just part of their everyday being now and everyday language. A lot of them choose to draw in their free time. A lot of them are noting things down in their free time. We've allowed them to draw quite a high-level awareness of literary devices and the language that authors use and the choices that authors make. And I think that that's such a huge skill and such a high-level skill that was just not being tapped into before. I also think just giving them the skill to be able to explore different characters and different palettes and different skin colours has been something they've really, really enjoyed. When working on Lucy Farfort's* In Our Hands *(2022) they spent a lot of time building up that colour palette and looking at focusing on the details. I think this level of detail is definitely reflected in their own writing and their own reading. They have that confidence now to create a character that is authentic and is reflective of themselves.*

> **Senior leader**

MEANINGFUL ENGAGEMENT WITH PROFESSIONAL AUTHORS/ILLUSTRATORS AND EMULATING AUTHENTIC AUTHORIAL PROCESSES

There is a real value in having the opportunity to meet authors, illustrators and poets. Author visits can be a source of excitement and inspiration. By meeting the face behind the book, children experience the heady mix of celebrity and opportunity to demystify the magic of writing a book. It can inspire a buzz around reading and an enthusiasm for writing. However, to solely engage authors on special occasions or one-off assemblies can risk reducing their contribution to a bit of entertainment, resulting in an immensely untapped resource. Creating opportunities for children to have the time to unpick, emulate and adapt the authentic creative process of an author deepens the scope of what such engagement can inspire.

> *I don't think that most of my children could name anyone really. I mean, maybe at a push, Michael Rosen, just because that's something that's kind of touched on every single year. But yes, I've definitely noticed children being able to name authors much, much more effectively talking about the style of authors more effectively. And most of the authors that they're talking about now are authors of colour, which I think is brilliant. And I think children also are more receptive to choosing an author that they respond to and that they have connection with.*

> **Class teacher**

This is a large part of the rationale for producing freely accessible short author videos to support the work we do at CLPE. These videos are key in offering insights into the authentic creative processes of authors, illustrators and poets for both teachers and children. By contemplating how professional authors work and giving children space to adopt and adapt such practices, we elevate them to the level of the professional. Through this meaningful and deeper level of engagement, we give them the tools and allow opportunity for experimentation to support them in broadening their toolkit and, in the process, finding ways that work for them. It also helps them to identify and hone their writing voice and style to fit the purpose and intended audience. They cease to write to the constraints of formulas or overly prescribed formats and instead write to communicate, they write with intention, conviction, enthusiasm and purpose, giving them a healthy sense of autonomy as learners.

OUR APPROACH TO LITERACY TEACHING

When combined these elements that define the CLPE approach to literacy teaching support teachers to empower children to have the autonomy and confidence to embrace and invest in their learning journey. This creates a crucial shift in the dynamic in the learning culture from children who might be passive compliant learners to children who are enthused, creative learners, hungry for knowledge and the opportunity to share ideas and thinking.

As teachers we have an enormous responsibility and power to influence and shape the next generation. We know that being literate influences the academic and socio-economic trajectory of each child. The power of reading lies in its capacity to move hearts, inspire spirits and shape minds. The power of writing is grounded in its potential to influence the world we live in and how we move forward as a society. Through the books and creatives we expose our children to we empower them to contribute to making the future the best that it can be for themselves and the wider world. So, what starts with today's book corner ends with a tomorrow that is a better, more inclusive and hopeful place to be.

The word is validated. Our parents feel validated and that's so important. It just helps build a stronger school community. And you know what? We can actually sense it. And it sounds such a cliché but it's books. It's the power of books.

Senior leader

RESOURCES

Our Reflecting Realities annual surveys and classroom-based action research form the basis of our advocacy work. These initiatives have been designed to promote inclusive practices and better representation in the education and publishing sectors. This work does not exist in isolation and in fact seeks to contribute to a much broader collective enterprise. We are fully aware that meaningful and long-lasting change requires a multi-layered, multi-faceted approach. It is only through the efforts and commitment of the many parents, teachers, librarians, booksellers, researchers, third sector organisations, funders and publishers that we will truly achieve the change we hope for. In this section, we have listed some of the organisations working in this area.

BOOKSELLERS CHAMPIONING A WIDE RANGE OF DIVERSE AND INCLUSIVE BOOKS

Afrori Books: afroribooks.co.uk

Book Love: www.thisisbooklove.com/

Letterbox Library: www.letterboxlibrary.com/

Lighthouse: lighthousebookshop.com/

Little Box of Books: littleboxofbooks.co.uk/

Moon Lane Books: www.moonlaneink.co.uk/

New Beacon Books: www.newbeaconbooks.com/

Newham Bookshop: www.newhambooks.co.uk/

News from Nowhere: www.newsfromnowhere.org.uk/

Round Table Books: www.roundtablebooks.co.uk/

The Willesden Bookshop: www.willesdenbookshop.co.uk/

Woke Babies: wokebabies.com/

ORGANISATIONS MAKING SPACE AND CREATING OPPORTUNITIES FOR CREATORS OF COLOUR

All Stories: www.allstories.org.uk/

BookTrust Represents: www.booktrust.org.uk/what-we-do/programmes-and-campaigns/booktrust-represents/#!?q=&sortOption=MostRecent&pageNo=1

Inclusive Books for Children Book Award: www.inclusivebooksforchidlren.org/awards

Jericho Prize: www.jerichoprize.com/

Jhalak Prize: www.jhalakprize.com/

Literature Wales: www.literaturewales.org/our-projects/representing-wales/

Lit in Colour: litincolour.penguin.co.uk/

Megaphone: megaphonewrite.com/megaphone-mentoring/

Speaking Volumes: speaking-volumes.org.uk/

Spread the Word: www.spreadtheword.org.uk/

Storymix: www.storymix.co.uk/

The Good Literacy Agency: www.thegoodliteraryagency.org/

RESEARCH, SURVEYS AND REPORTS THAT GIVE US IMPORTANT INFORMATION ABOUT REPRESENTATION IN CHILDREN'S LITERATURE AND THE PUBLISHING INDUSTRY

CILIP Carnegie and Kate Greenaway Awards Independent Diversity Review Final Report (2018): cdn.ymaws.com/www.cilip.org.uk/resource/resmgr/cilip/information_profes sional_and_news/press_releases/2018_09_ckgfinalreport/cilip_ckg_diversity_review_f.pdf

Chantiluke, R., Courtney, M., Elliott, V. and Nelson-Addy, L. (2021) *Lit in Colour: Diversity in Literature in English Schools.* Co-commissioned by Penguin Random House and the Runnymede Trust: litincolour.penguin.co.uk/#group-section-About-Lit-in-Colour-J3ZIrTsrhw

Diversity Survey of the Publishing Workforce 2020: www.publishers.org.uk/publications/diversity-survey-of-the-publishing-workforce-2020/

Harris, C., Leather, D. and Stiell, B. (2019) *Time for Change Black and Minority Ethnic Representation in the Children's Literature Sector. A Report for Arts Council England.* Sheffield Hallam University: www.artscouncil.org.uk/sites/default/files/download-file/04-11-19% 20Time%20for%20Change%20-%20Research%20Report%20FINAL.pdf

Ramdarshan Bold, M.R. (2019) *BookTrust Represents: Representation of People of Colour among Children's Book Authors and Illustrators*: www.booktrust.org.uk/what-we-do/programmes-and-campaigns/booktrust-represents/representation-of-people-of-colour-among-childrens-book-authors-and-illustrators/?q=&sortOption=MostRecent&pageNo=1#!?q=&sortOption=MostRecent&pageNo=1

Saha, A. and Van Lente, S. (2020) *Rethinking 'Diversity' in Publishing*. London: Goldsmiths Press: www.spreadtheword.org.uk/wp-content/uploads/2020/06/Rethinking_diversity_in-publishing_WEB.pdf

ORGANISATIONS PROVIDING RESOURCES AND OPPORTUNITIES FOR SCHOOLS TO DEVELOP THEIR PROVISION IN THIS AREA

British Library: www.bl.uk/childrens-books

The Black Curriculum: theblackcurriculum.com/

Royal African Society: royalafricansociety.org/whatwedo/education/poetry-in-the-primary-classroom/

BIBLIOGRAPHY

WEBSITES

BookTrust Represents: www.booktrust.org.uk/what-we-do/programmes-and-campaigns/book-trust-represents/representation-of-people-of-colour-among-childrens-book-authors-and-illustrators/?q=&sortOption=MostRecent&pageNo=1#!?q=&sortOption=MostRecent&pageNo=1

CLPE Corebooks Online: clpe.org.uk/books/corebooks/corebooks-collections

CLPE (2016) The Reading Scale: clpe.org.uk/library-and-resources/reading-and-writing-scales

CLPE Reflecting Realities Annual Surveys: clpe.org.uk/research/reflecting-realities

Cooperative Children's Book Center School of Education University of Wisconsin-Madison: ccbc.education.wisc.edu/literature-resources/ccbc-diversity-statistics/

BOOKS, JOURNAL ARTICLES AND PUBLICATIONS

Abdi, F., Anders, J., Barnard, M., Frerichs, J., Shure, N. and Wyse, D. (2021) *Education Endowment Funded Evaluation Report of CLPE's Power of Pictures*. London: EEF.

Abdi, M. (2022) *Somali Student's Experiences: Masculinity, Race and Identity*. Switzerland: Palgrave Macmillan.

Adeola, D. (2021) *Hey You!: An Empowering Celebration of Growing Up Black*. London: Puffin.

Adeola, D. (ed.) (2022) *Joyful, Joyful: Stories Celebrating Black Voices*. London: Two Hoots.

Agbabi, P. (2020) *The Infinite: 1 (The Leap Cycle)*. London: Canongate.

Ahmed, S. (2020) *Noor Inayat Khan*. UK: Scholastic.

Ahmed, S. (2022) *Princess Sophia Duleep Singh*. UK: Scholastic.

Alexander, K. (2016) *Booked*. London: Houghton Mifflin Harcourt and Rights People.

Alexander, K. (2018) *Rebound*. New York: Houghton Mifflin Harcourt.

Alexander, K. (2023) *An American Story*. Boston, MA: Little Brown.

Alexander, K. (2023) *The Door of No Return*. London: Andersen Press.

Alexander, K. (2023) *Why Fathers Cry at Night: A Memoir in Love Poems, Recipes, Letters, and Remembrances*. Boston, MA: Little Brown.

Alexander, K. and Nelson, K. (Illustrator) (2020) *The Undefeated*. London: Andersen Press.

Alexander, K. and Patterson, J. (2020) *Becoming Muhammad Ali*. London: Hatchette.

Anders, J., Shure, N., Wyse, D., Barnard, M., Abdi, F. and Frerichs, J. (2021) *Evaluation Report: The Power of Pictures*. London: EEF.

Atta, D., Coelho, J., Getten, K., Lawrence, P., Lola, T., Norry, E.L., Richards, J., Sheppard, A. and Sode, Y. (2021) *Happy Here: 10 Stories from Black British Authors and Illustrators*. London: Knights Of.

Barrs, M. and Cork, V. (2001) *The Reader in the Writer*. London: Centre for Literacy in Primary Education (CLPE).

Barrs, M., Ellis, S. and Blake, Q. (Illustrator) (1996) *The Core Book: Structured Approach to Using Books within the Reading Curriculum*. London: CLPE.

Benjamin, F., Chimbiri, K.N., Norry, E.L., Hepburn, J., Massey, K., Godden, S., Jackman, J, Quincey the Comedian, George, K., Latoya, K. and Hickson-Lovence, A. (2021) *The Place for Me: Stories About the Windrush Generation*. UK: Scholastic.

Bishop, R.S. (1990) *Mirrors, Windows and Sliding Doors*. Perspectives, *6* (3), pp. ix–xi.

Blackman, M. and Adeola, D. (2021) *We're Going to Find the Monster!* London: Puffin.

Bloom, V. and Wilson-Max, K. (Illustrator) (2021) *Stars with Flaming Tails: Poems*. UK: Otter-Barry.

Bryon, N. and Adeola, D. (Ilustrator)(2019) *Look Up!* London: Puffin.

Bryon, N. and Adeola, D. (Ilustrator)(2020a) *Clean Up!* London: Puffin.

Bryon, N. and Adeola, D. (Ilustrator)(2020b) *Speak Up!* London: Puffin

Chambers, A. (2011) *Tell Me: Children, Reading and Talk with the Reading Environment*. Stroud: Thimble Press.

Chan, M. and Cao, A. (Illustrator) (2021) *Danny Chung Does Not Do Maths*. London: Piccadilly Press.

Chantiluke, R., Courtney, M., Elliott, V. and Nelson-Addy, L. (2021) *Lit in Colour: Diversity in Literature in English Schools*. Co-commissioned by Penguin Random House and the Runnymede Trust.

Cheng, W., Chunhe, L., Feng, J., Jiang, Y., Kang, J., Langley, C., Li, C., Sahakian, B.J., Sun, Y., Yang, A. and Zhao, X. (2023) *Early-initiated Childhood Reading for Pleasure: Associations with Better Cognitive Performance, Mental Well-being and Brain Structure in Young Adolescence*. Published online by Cambridge University Press.

Chetty, D. (2016) You can't say that! Stories have to be about white people. *The Good Immigrant*. Unbound, pp. 96–107.

Chetty, D., Golding, A. and Rollock, N. (2022) Reimagining education: Where do we go from here?, *Wasafiri*, *37* (4), pp. 1–3. DOI: 10.1080/02690055.2022.2104475

Chetty, D. and Sands-O'Connor, K. (2020) *Books for Keeps: Beyond the Secret Garden? Classic Literature and Classic Mistakes*. booksforkeeps.co.uk/article/beyond-the-secret-garden-classic-literature-and-classic-mistakes/

CLPE (2018) *Reflecting Realities: Survey of Ethnic Representation within UK Children's Literature 2017*. London: CLPE.

CLPE (2019) *Reflecting Realities: Survey of Ethnic Representation within UK Children's Literature 2018*. London: CLPE.

CLPE (2020a) *Reflecting Realities: Survey of Ethnic Representation within UK Children's Literature 2019*. London: CLPE.

CLPE (2020b) *The Power of a Rich Reading Classroom*. UK: Corwin.

CLPE (2021) *Reflecting Realities: Survey of Ethnic Representation within UK Children's Literature 2020*. London: CLPE.

CLPE (2022) *Reflecting Realities: Survey of Ethnic Representation within UK Children's Literature 2017–2022* (November). London: CLPE.

Coelho, J. (2014) *Werewolf Club Rules*. London: Frances Lincoln.

Coelho, J. (2017) *How to Write Poems*. London: Bloomsbury.

Coelho, J. (2017) *Overheard in a Tower Block*. Hereford: Otter-Barry.

Coelho, J. (2018) *If All the World Were …* London: Lincoln Children's.

Coelho, J. (2019) *The Girl Who Became a Tree*. Hereford: Otter-Barry.

Coelho, J. and Hartas, F. (Illustrator) (2020) *Zombierella: Fairy Tales Gone Bad*. London: Walker.

Coelho, J. (2022) *The Boy Lost in the Maze*. Hereford: Otter-Barry.

Cremin, T. (2020) Reading for pleasure: Challenges and opportunities. In Davison, J. and Daly, C. (eds), *Debates in English Teaching*. London: Routledge.

Deen, S. and Sarkar, A. (Illustrator) (2020) *Agent Asha: Mission Shark Bytes*. London: Walker.

Department for Education (DfE) (1975) *A Language for Life: Report of the Committee of Enquiry appointed by the Secretary of State for Education and Science under the Chairmanship of Sir Alan Bullock FBA*. London: DfE.

DfE (2013) *The National Curriculum in England Key Stages 1 and 2 Framework Document*. London: DfE.

Drury, F.K.W. (1930) *Book Selection*. Chicago: ALA.

Ellis, S., Barrs, M. and Blake, Q. (1996) *The Core Book: Structured Approach to Using Books within the Reading Curriculum*. London: CLPE.

Farfort, L. (2022) *In Our Hands*. London: Tate.

Friere, P. (1996) *Pedagogy of the Oppressed*. Myra Bergman Ramose (Translator). London: Penguin.

Gavin, J. and Collingridge, R. (Illustrator) (2014) *Blackberry Blue: And Other Fairy Tales*. UK: Tamarind.

Getten, K. (2021) *Two Sisters: A Story of Freedom*. UK: Scholastic.

Gilbert, L., Teravainen, A., Clark, C. and Shaw, S. (2018) *Literacy and Life Expectancy: An Evidence Review Exploring the Link between Literacy and Life Expectancy in England through Health and Socioeconomic Factors*. London: National Literacy Trust.

Haddow, S. (2021a) *My Dad is a Grizzly Bear*. London: Macmillan.

Haddow, S. (2021b) *Torn Apart: The Partition of India, 1947*. UK: Scholastic.

Haddow, S. (2022) *My Mum is a Lioness*. London: Macmillan.

Ho-Yen, P. (2015) *Boy in the Tower*. UK: Corgi Children's.

Hodgson Burnett, F. and Bailey, P. (2016) *The Secret Garden*. UK: Alma.

Huq, K. (2020) *Cookie!: Cookie and the Most Annoying Boy in the World*. London: Piccadilly Press.

Islam, B. and Khandaker, F. (Illustrator) (2021) *Mayhem Mission*. London: Knights Of.

Jackson, S. (2019) *High-Rise Mystery*. London: Knights Of.

Johnson, C. (2013) *Sawbones*. London: Walker.

Johnson, C. (2018) *Freedom*. UK: Scholastic.

Johnson, C. and Sanson, R. (Illustrator) (2020) *To Liberty! The Adventures of Thomas-Alexandre Dumas*. UK: Bloomsbury.

Johnson, C. and Hickey, K. (Illustrator) (2021) *Race to the Frozen North: The Matthew Henson Story*. UK: Barrington Stoke.

Johnson, C. and Hickey, K. (Illustrator) (2022) *Journey Back to Freedom: The Olaudah Equiano Story*. UK: Barrington Stoke.

Krashen, S.D. (2004) *The Power of Reading: Insights from the Research*. USA: Heinemann.

Lander, V. (ed.) (2018) *Fundamental British Values*. Oxfordshire: Routledge.

Lawrence, P. (2016) *Orangeboy*. London: Hatchette.

Lawrence, P. (2019) *Diver's Daughter: A Tudor Story*. UK: Scholastic.

Lawrence, P. (2022a) *The Elemental Detectives*. UK: Scholastic.

Lawrence, P. (2022b) *Needle*. Edinburgh: Barrington Stoke.

Mann, M. (2020) *Run Rebel*. London: Penguin.

Mann, M. (2021) *The Crossing*. London: Penguin.

Mann, M. (2022) *Small's Big Dreams*. London: HarperCollins.

McQuinn, A. and Beardshaw, R. (Illustrator) (2017) *Lulu Gets a Cat*. UK: Alanna Max.

McQuinn, A. and Beardshaw, R. (Illustrator) (2019) *Lulu's First Day*. UK: Alanna Max.

McQuinn, A. and Beardshaw, R. (Illustrator) (2021) *Lulu Loves Flowers*. UK: Alanna Max.

McQuinn, A. and Beardshaw, R. (Illustrator) (2021) *Lulu's Sleepover*. UK: Alanna Max.

McQuinn, A. and Hearson, R. (Illustrator) (2021) *Zeki Can Swim*. UK: Alanna Max.

McQuinn, A. and Hearson, R. (Illustrator) (2021) *Zeki Gets a Checkup*. UK: Alanna Max.

McQuinn, A. and Hearson, R. (Illustrator) (2022) *Zeki Sleep Tight*. UK: Alanna Max.

Meek, M. (1987) *How Texts Teach What Readers Learn*. Stroud: Thimble Press.

Mian, Z. and Mafaridik, N. (Illustrator) (2019) *Accidental Trouble Magnet*. London: Hodder.

National Literacy Trust (2022) *Working Together Towards a Library in Every Primary School: An update from the Primary School Library Alliance*. London: National Literacy Trust.

Norry, E.L. (2019) *Son of the Circus: A Victorian Story*. UK: Scholastic.

Norry, E.L. (2021) *Amber Undercover*. Oxford: Oxford University Press.

Norry, E.L. (2023) *Fablehouse*. London: Bloomsbury.

Norry, E.L. and Chow, S. (2021) *Lionel Messi*. UK: Scholastic.

Norry, E.L. (Author) and Evans, A. (Illustrator) (2021) *The Extraordinary Life of Nelson Mandela: Lektüre*. London: Puffin.

Ofsted (2022) *Research Review Series: English*. www.gov.uk/government/publications/curriculum-research-review-series-english/curriculum-research-review-series-english

Olusoga, D. (2020) *Black and British: A Short, Essential History*. London: Macmillan.

Olusoga, D., Alexander, J. (Illustrator) and Taylor, M. (Illustrator) (2021) *Black and British: An Illustrated History*. London: Macmillan.

O'Neill, R. (2023) *A Different Kind of Freedom: A Romani Story*. UK: Scholastic.

Patel, S. and McCann, E. (Illustrator) (2020) *Anisha, Accidental Detective*. London: Usborne.

Patel, S. and Stevens, R. (eds) (2021) *The Very Merry Murder Club*. London: Farshore.

Rai, B. (2019) *Now or Never: A Dunkirk Story*. UK: Scholastic.

Ramdarshan Bold, M.R. (2019) *Representation of People of Colour Among Children's Book Authors and Illustrators*. London: BookTrust.

Rasheed, L. (2020) *Empire's End: A Roman Story*. UK: Scholastic.

Rauf, O. (2018) *The Boy at the Back of the Class*. London: Orion.

Rosen, M. (2017) *A Great Big Cuddle: Poems for the Very Young*. London: Walker.

Rosen, M. (2021) The Missing: The True Story of My Family in World War II. London: Walker.

Rosen, M. and Blake, Q. (Illustrator) (2022) *On The Move: Poems About Migration*. London: Walker.

Said, S.F. and Mckean, D. (Illustrator) (2014) *Varjak Paw*. London: Corgi Children's.

Said, S.F. and Mckean, D. (Illustrator) (2022) *Tyger*. London: David Fickling.

Sims Bishop, R. (1990) Mirrors, windows and sliding glass doors. *Perspectives: Choosing and Using Books for the Classroom, 6* (3).

Sullivan, A. and Brown, M. (2015) Reading for pleasure and progress in vocabulary and mathematics. *British Educational Research Journal, 41* (6).

Sun, Y., Sahakian, B., Langley, C., Yang, A., Jiang, Y., Kang, J. and Feng, J. (2023) Early-initiated childhood reading for pleasure: Associations with better cognitive performance, mental wellbeing and brain structure in young adolescence. *Psychological Medicine*, pp. 1–15.

The Reading Agency (2015) *Literature Review: The Impact of Reading for Pleasure and Empowerment*. UK: BOP Consulting.

Thomas, E.E. (2019) *The Dark Fantastic: Race and the Imagination from Harry Potter to the Hunger Games*. USA: NYU Press.

Wilkins, V. (2008) *Patrick Hardy Lecture: The Right to be Seen*. UK: Tamarind.

Wilson-Max, K. (2020) *Where's Lenny?* UK: Alanna Max.

Yousafzai, M. and Kerascoët (Illustrator) (2019) *Malala's Magic Pencil*. London: Puffin.

Zephaniah, B. (2020) *Windrush Child*. UK: Scholastic.

INDEX